Heirs with Christ

Heirs with Christ:
The Puritans on Adoption

Joel R. Beeke

REFORMATION HERITAGE BOOKS
Grand Rapids, Michigan

Published by
Reformation Heritage Books
2965 Leonard St., NE
Grand Rapids, MI 49525
616-977-0599 / Fax 616-285-3246
e-mail: orders@heritagebooks.org
website: www.heritagebooks.org

Scriptural quotations are taken from the King James Version.

This book is an expanded version of the chapter
"Transforming Power and Comfort: The Puritans on
Adoption," in *The Faith Once Delivered: Celebrating
the Legacy of Reformed Systematic Theology and the
Westminster Assembly,* edited by Anthony Selvaggio
(Philipsburg, N.J.: P & R, 2007), pages 63–105.

Library of Congress Cataloging-in-Publication Data

Beeke, Joel R., 1952-
  Heirs with Christ : the Puritans on adoption / Joel R. Beeke.
     p. cm.
  Includes bibliographical references and index.
  ISBN 978-1-60178-040-9 (pbk. : alk. paper)
  1. Adoption (Theology) 2. Puritans--Doctrines. I. Title.
  BX9323.B44 2008
  234--dc22
                              2008012657

*For additional Reformed literature, both new and used,
request a free book list from Reformation Heritage Books
at the above address.*

———◆◆◆———

With gratitude for

Lois Haley

diligent and loyal friend, typist,
and book-packer, who has shipped out
millions of dollars worth of books
with a prayer in her heart
for their divine benediction

———◆◆◆———

"We have enough in us to move God to correct us, but nothing to move him to adopt us, therefore exalt free grace, begin the work of angels here; bless him with your praises who hath blessed you in making you his sons and daughters."

– Thomas Watson
A Body of Divinity
(London: A. Fullarton, 1845)

Contents

Foreword

Earthly adoption is *horizontal*. It is one human being establishing a relationship with another human being. Heavenly adoption is *vertical*. It is the eternal God graciously establishing a relationship with fallen human beings, creatures who are by nature "children of disobedience" (Eph. 2:2) or "children of wrath" (Eph. 2:3).

God is an adoptive Father. Jesus, our Elder Brother, is God the Father's eternal, only-begotten, natural Son. We believers are His children through adoption. This identity is central to who we are. As adopted children, we enjoy all the rights and privileges of the relationship that God the Father enjoys with His eternal Son. This is an amazing reality and eternal privilege.

Adoption is heavenly before it is earthly. One is what God does; the other is what we do. Adoption is something God has done and is doing before it is something we have done and are doing. Adoption was invented by God even before He created the world. Adoption is how God brings us into His family.

If adoption is first heavenly before it is earthly, why do we Christians so often think of earthly adoption before we think of heavenly adoption? Why do we think horizontally before we think vertically? I think one reason for this is the neglect of the doctrine of adoption in the history of the church. In his massive, 2,600-page work *The Creeds of Christendom*, the church historian Philip Schaff only includes six creeds that contain a section on adoption because they are the only ones he could find while scouring almost 1,900 years of church history.

The early church was primarily concerned, and rightly so, with the doctrines of the Trinity and of Christ because those doctrines were being attacked within the church. The Reformation and post-Reformation church necessarily focused on defending the doctrine of justification. These battles were all essential for the church to fight in the defense of Christian truth, but unintentionally they resulted in the church's failure thoroughly to develop Scripture's teaching on adoption.

Even though adoption has been relatively neglected in the history of the church, the Puritans have not contributed to that neglect. To my knowledge, no tradition in the history of the church has rejoiced in and proclaimed the truth of adoption as have the Puritans. Though the Puritans, as of late, have received bad press in their treatment of this great doctrine, their writings demonstrate that they esteemed nothing higher than the incomparable privilege of being God's children through adoption.

Dr. Joel Beeke offers a great service to the contemporary church by examining the Puritans' substantial and worship-filled treatment of the believer's adoption by God. Beeke does a masterful job of setting the record straight on behalf of the Puritans. He has extensively studied the Puritans and is uniquely qualified to write on this most important subject.

The church today should richly benefit from this exposure to Puritan teaching on the biblical doctrine of adoption. If we as Christians even begin to approach the Puritans' love of heavenly adoption, we will be spiritually richer for it. Therefore, I highly recommend Dr. Beeke's book *Heirs with Christ: The Puritans on Adoption.*

—Dan Cruver
    Co-Founder of Together
    for Adoption

Acknowledgments

I owe thanks most of all to the glorious God and Father for adopting me:

- decretally, from eternity;
- meritoriously, based on the justifying power of Christ's death and resurrection;
- objectively, through regenerating me in Yellowstone National Park in the summer of 1967;
- consciously, through a pastoral visit by Rev. Arie Elshout to our family in 1969 that the Spirit used to assure me of spiritual freedom; and
- daily, loading me, despite my sinfulness, with the unspeakably powerful comforts of His adopting benefits and grace.

I am deeply grateful to the Puritans who showed me the theological riches and beauties of adoption as no other writers have done. This study of Puritans on adoption has blessed me more than any other, except perhaps my study of the assurance of faith.

I offer heartfelt thanks for my wonderful family and the love that we share. That love moves me to contemplate my spiritual adoption with tears. I often ask my children, "Do you know what your dad thinks of you?" When they respond with cheerful confidence, "You love me," I ask God for grace once again to approach Him likewise as my heavenly Father. Sometimes I pester my children further, asking, "But

how do you know?" I want to hear them say something like this: "You tell me and you show me, so I
know it and I feel it." "Lord," I then cry out, "Thou
dost tell me in Thy Word, dost witness to my heart,
and dost show me in a thousand ways Thy paternal
love toward me. *Soli Deo Gloria!*" Just as I don't
deserve my special wife, Mary, or such special children as Calvin, Esther, and Lydia, how much less do
I deserve such a God as my heavenly Father is to me
in Christ Jesus. I am unworthy of my God and my
family, but that indebtedness makes me appreciate
the doctrine of loving adoption more than ever.

I thank Jay Collier for his detailed work with the
manuscript that turned into this book; Dan Cruver,
for his foreword; Phyllis TenElshof, Kate DeVries,
and Martha Fisher for their editing; Linda den Hol-
lander for her typesetting; and Amy Zevenbergen for
her work on the cover.

If this little book, with the blessing of the Spirit,
helps God-fearing believers more fully lay hold of the
Father's love to them in Christ Jesus, my reward will
be multiplied. I believe that if God's people were conscious every day that they are adopted by the Father,
Spirit-worked revival would break out and the exqui-
site delight believers would have in their Father in
heaven would move the world profoundly.

Heavenly Father, stir up Thy people to understand, believe, receive, and taste with delight Thy
amazing Fatherhood.

—Joel R. Beeke

———————— ◆ ————————

CHAPTER ONE

Introduction:
Correcting a Caricature

Reformed theologians in general, and the Puritans in particular, have gotten a bad press for their supposed lack of teaching on adoption, that is, the biblical doctrine that every true Christian is God's adopted child. In his otherwise excellent chapter titled "Sons of God" in the classic, *Knowing God,* J. I. Packer writes, "Adoption has been little regarded in Christian history. Apart from two last-century books, now scarcely known (R. S. Candlish, *The Fatherhood of God,* R. A. Webb, *The Reformed Doctrine of Adoption*), there is no evangelical writing on it, nor has there been at any time since the Reformation, any more than there was before.... The Puritan teaching on the Christian life, so strong in other ways, was notably deficient [on adoption], which is one reason why legalistic misunderstandings of it so easily arise."[1] As recently

---

1. J. I. Packer, *Knowing God* (Downers Grove, Ill.: InterVarsity, 1973), 207.

as 1993, Douglas Kelly concurs: "As James I. Packer noted several years ago in *Knowing God,* Reformed Christians have failed to work through the doctrine of Adoption."[2] Statements such as these promote the familiar comment that adoption is *the* neglected aspect in the Reformed *ordo salutis.*

Such generalizations have found a degree of confirmation in the minimal attention that many Reformed systematic theologies give to adoption. For example, George Hill, Charles Hodge, W. G. T. Shedd, Robert L. Dabney, Louis Berkhof, and G. Henry Kersten, devote only one or two paragraphs to adoption at best. But this is by no means universally the case.[3] William Ames, Francis Turretin, John Brown of Haddington, James Boyce, A. A. Hodge, and Robert Reymond provide a more ample treatment of adoption (4–6 pages).[4] Better yet, Thomas Watson,

---

2. Douglas Kelly, "Adoption: An Underdeveloped Heritage of the Westminster Standards," *Reformed Theological Review* 52 (1993): 111.

3. Erroll Hulse exaggerates when he asserts that most systematic theologians have ignored adoption ("Recovering the Doctrine of Adoption," *Reformation Today* 105 [1988]:10).

4. William Ames, *The Marrow of Theology,* trans. and ed. John D. Eusden (Boston: Pilgrim Press, 1968), 164–67; Francis Turretin, *Institutes of Elenctic Theology,* trans. George Musgrave Giger, ed. James T. Dennison, Jr. (Phillipsburg, N.J.: P & R, 1994), 2:666–69; John Brown, *The Systematic Theology of John Brown of Haddington* (Grand Rapids: Reformation Heritage Books, 2002), 393–97; James P. Boyce, *Abstract of Systematic Theology* (reprint, Hanford, Calif.: den Dulk Christian Foundation, n.d.), 404–409; A. A. Hodge, *Outlines of Theology* (reprint, Edinburgh:

Samuel Willard, John Dick, Timothy Dwight, John Gill, James Boice, and Wayne Grudem provide rather full treatments ranging from 6–20 pages.[5] Most thorough, however, are Herman Witsius, *The Economy of the Covenants Between God & Man* (28 pages), and Robert Breckinridge, *The Knowledge of God, Subjectively Considered* (25 pages)—in fact, Breckinridge devotes more pages to adoption than to any other aspect of the *ordo salutis!*[6] And, of course, let us not forget John Calvin, whose repeated references to adoption permeate his entire theology and "the whole

---

Banner of Truth Trust, 1986), 515–19; Robert L. Reymond, *A New Systematic Theology of the Christian Faith* (Nashville: Thomas Nelson, 1998), 759–62.

5. Thomas Watson, *A Body of Divinity in a Series of Sermons on the Shorter Catechism* (London: A. Fullarton, 1845), 155–60; Samuel Willard, *A Compleat Body of Divinity* (reprint, New York: Johnson Reprint Corporation, 1969), 482–91; John Dick, *Lectures on Theology* (Philadelphia: J. Whetham & Son, 1841), 2:224–33; Timothy Dwight, *Theology: Explained and Defended, in a Series of Sermons* (Middletown, Conn.: Clark & Lyman, 1818), 3:181–93; John Gill, *A Complete Body of Doctrinal and Practical Divinity* (reprint, Paris, Ark.: Baptist Standard Bearer, 1987), 201–203, 518–25; James M. Boice, *Foundations of the Christian Faith: A Comprehensive & Readable Theology* (Downers Grove, Ill.: InterVarsity Press, 1986), 441–48; Wayne Grudem, *Systematic Theology: An Introduction to Biblical Doctrine* (Grand Rapids: Zondervan, 1994), 736–45.

6. Herman Witsius, *The Economy of the Covenants* (reprint, Kingsburg, Calif.: den Dulk Christian Foundation, 1990), 1:441–68; Robert J. Breckinridge, *The Knowledge of God, Subjectively Considered* (New York: Robert Carter & Brothers, 1859), 178–202.

ethos of the Christian life," despite his lack of appor-
tioning it a specific section in the *Institutes*.[7]

In addition to systematic theologies, the subject
of adoption has been addressed from a Reformed
perspective at length in several nineteenth-century
treatises in addition to Candlish and Webb, mentioned
by Packer above. Thomas Crawford's *The Fatherhood
of God* responds to Candlish's denial of the univer-
sal paternity of God.[8] In his *Discussion of Theological
Questions,* John L. Girardeau devotes nearly one
hundred pages to the doctrine of adoption—first

---

7. John Calvin, *Institutes of the Christian Religion*, trans. Ford
Lewis Battles, ed. John T. McNeill (Philadelphia: Westminster
Press, 1960); Sinclair B. Ferguson, "The Reformed Doctrine of
Sonship," in *Pulpit and People: Essays in Honour of William Still
on his 75th Birthday*, ed. Nigel M. de S. Cameron and Sinclair B.
Ferguson (Edinburgh: Rutherford House Books, 1986), 84. For
a thorough study of Calvin on adoption, see Tim J. R. Trumper,
"An Historical Study of the Doctrine of Adoption in the Calvinistic
Tradition" (Ph.D. dissertation, University of Edinburgh, 2001),
38–214.

8. Robert S. Candlish, *The Fatherhood of God,* 2nd ed.
(Edinburgh: Adam and Charles Black, 1865)—see also his
*Discourses bearing upon the Sonship and Brotherhood of
Believers and other kindred subjects* (Edinburgh: Adam and
Charles Black, 1872); Robert S. Webb, *The Reformed Doctrine
of Adoption* (reprint, Grand Rapids: Eerdmans, 1947)—see also
his *Christian Salvation: Its Doctrine and Experience* (Richmond,
Va.: Presbyterian Committee of Publication, 1921), 391–405, and
"The Fatherhood of God," *Presbyterian Quarterly* 5 (1891):56–
70; Thomas Crawford, *The Fatherhood of God Considered in Its
General and Special Aspects and Particularly in Relation to the
Atonement with a Review of Recent Speculations on the Subject*,
3rd ed. (Edinburgh: William Blackwood and Sons, 1868).

responding to the Candlish-Crawford debate, then setting forth his own understanding.[9] In my opinion, Thomas Houston's *The Adoption of Sons* is superior to all of these volumes and has been unduly ignored in secondary literature on the subject.[10]

The twentieth century saw a burst of evangelical writings on adoption, including several popular books by solidly Reformed men such as Sinclair Ferguson, Mark Johnston, and Robert Peterson.[11] Scores of articles in academic journals were published on adoption,[12] and at least seven Ph.D. and Th.M. dis-

---

9. John L. Girardeau, *Discussion of Theological Questions,* ed. George A. Blackburn (reprint, Harrisonburg, Va.: Sprinkle Publications, 1986), 428–521. For an able exposition of Girardeau's views, see Stephen R. Berry, "'Sons of God': An Examination of the Doctrine of Adoption in the Thought of John Lafayette Girardeau" (unpublished paper submitted to systematic theology department, Reformed Theological Seminary [Jackson, Miss.], 1994). Berry also addresses the views of Candlish, Crawford, and Thornwell.

10. Thomas Houston, *The Adoption of Sons, Its Nature, Spirit, Privileges, and Effects: A Practical and Experimental Treatise* (Edinburgh: Alex. Gardner, Paisley, 1872).

11. Sinclair B. Ferguson, *Children of the Living God* (Edinburgh: Banner of Truth Trust, 1989); Mark Johnston, *Child of a King: The Biblical Doctrine of Sonship* (Fearn, Rosshire: Christian Focus, 1997); Robert Peterson, *Adopted by God: From Wayward Sinners to Cherished Children* (Phillipsburg, N.J.: P & R Publishing, 2001) — see also his "Toward a Systematic Theology of Adoption," *Presbyterion* 27, no. 2 (Fall 2001): 120–31.

12. E.g., James Barr, "Abba Isn't Daddy." *Journal of Theological Studies* 39 (1988): 28–47; Trevor J. Burke, "Adoption and the Spirit in Romans 8," *Evangelical Quarterly* 70 (1998): 311–24, and "The Characteristics of Paul's Adoptive-Sonship *(Huiothesia)*

sertations contributed substantially to the subject.[13]

Motif," *Irish Biblical Studies* 17 (1995): 62–74; Herbert Donner, "Adoption oder Legitimation? Erwägungen zur Adoption im Alten Testament auf dem Hintergrund der altorientalischen Rechte," *Oriens Antiquus* 8 (1969): 87–119; Samuel Feigin, "Some Cases of Adoption in Israel," *Journal of Biblical Literature* 50 (1931): 186–200; W. A. Jarrel, "Adoption Not in the Bible Salvation," *The Review and Expositor* 15 (1918): 459–69; S. A. King, "The Grace of Adoption," *Union Seminary Magazine* 22 (1910): 30–35; Francis Lyall, "Roman Law in the Writings of Paul—Adoption," *Journal of Biblical Literature* 88 (1969): 458–66; Allen Mawhinney, "Baptism, Servanthood and Sonship," *Westminster Theological Journal* 49 (1987): 35–64—also "The Family of God: One Model for the Church of the 90s," *Presbyterion* 19, no. 2 (Fall 1993): 77–96, and "God as Father: Two Popular Theories Reconsidered," *Journal of the Evangelical Theological Society* 31 (1988): 181–89; Birgit Stolt, "Martin Luther on God as Father," *Lutheran Quarterly* 8 (1994): 385–95; James Swetnam, "On Romans 8:23 and the 'Expectation of Sonship,'" *Biblica* 48 (1967): 102–108; Daniel J. Theron, "'Adoption' in the Pauline Corpus," *Evangelical Quarterly* 28 (1956): 6–14; Tim J. R. Trumper, "The Metaphorical Import of Adoption: A Plea for Realisation I and II: The Adoption Metaphor in Biblical Usage," *Scottish Bulletin of Evangelical Theology* 14 (1996): 129–45; 15 (1997): 98–115; Nigel Westhead, "Adoption in the Thought of John Calvin," *Scottish Bulletin of Evangelical Theology* 13 (1995): 102–115; Thornton Whaling, "Adoption," *Princeton Theological Review* 21 (1923): 223–35; G. A. Wilterdink, "The Fatherhood of God in Calvin's Thought," *Reformed Review* 30 (Autumn 1976): 9–22; Bernard Woudenberg, "Eternal Adoption," *The Standard Bearer* (September 1, 1990), 475–77.

13. Frank J. Ebel, Jr., "The Christian's Filial Relationship to God" (Th.M. thesis, Dallas Theological Seminary, 1957); T. Scott Franchino, "*Yios* and *Teknon* in the Doctrine of Adoption: Romans 8" (Th.M. thesis, Grace Theological Seminary, Winona Lake., Ind., 1984); Allen Mawhinney, "*Huiothesia* in the Pauline Epistles: Its Background, Use, and Implications" (Ph.D. dissertation,

Already in the present century two major Ph.D. dissertations on adoption have been completed.[14]

But what about the Puritans? Is it correct to assert that "the Puritans did little in exploring this truth apart from a few paragraphs here and there"?[15]

The evidence suggests that adoption, though not developed as thoroughly as several closely knit doctrines such as justification, sanctification, and assurance, was certainly not a neglected topic among the Puritans. Treatment of the topic in the systematic theologies of William Ames, Thomas Watson, Samuel Willard, and Herman Witsius has already been noted. William Perkins, often denominated the father of Puritanism, addresses various aspects of adoption at some length in at least nine different

---

Baylor University, 1983); Keith Alan Mosebrook, "The Pauline Doctrine of the Adoption of Believers" (Th.M. thesis, Dallas Theological Seminary, 1981); Robert Lee Riffe, "A Study of the Figure of Adoption in the Pauline Epistles" (Th.M. thesis, Dallas Theological Seminary, 1981); Charles A. Wanamaker, "The Son and the Sons of God: A Study in Elements of Paul's Christologial and Soteriological Thought" (Ph.D. dissertation, University of Durham, 1980); Robert E. Wermuth, "The Doctrine of Adoption in Paul's Ephesian Letter" (Th.M. thesis, Covenant Theological Seminary, St. Louis, 1985).

14. Tim J. R. Trumper, "An Historical Study of the Doctrine of Adoption in the Calvinistic Tradition" (University of Edinburgh, 2001); David B. Garner, "Adoption in Christ" (Westminster Theological Seminary, 2002).

15. Erroll Hulse, "Recovering the Doctrine of Adoption," *Reformation Today* 105 (1988): 10.

places in his works.[16] William Bates, Hugh Binning, Thomas Brooks, Anthony Burgess, Stephen Charnock, George Downame, John Flavel, Thomas Goodwin, William Gouge, Ezekiel Hopkins, Edward Leigh, and John Owen all provide some treatment of the subject.[17] Other Puritans, such as Jeremiah Burroughs, Thomas Cole, Roger Drake, Thomas Hooker,

---

16. *The Workes of that Famovs and VVorthy Minister of Christ in the Vniuersitie of Cambridge, Mr. William Perkins,* 3 vols. (London: Iohn Legatt and Cantrell Ligge, 1612–13), 1:82–83, 104–105, 369–70, 430; 2:277–80; 3:154–55, 138, 205, and 382 of 2nd pagination.

17. William Bates, *The Whole Works of the Rev. W. Bates, D.D.,* ed. W. Farmer (reprint, Harrisonburg, Va.: Sprinkle, 1990, 4:299–301); Hugh Binning, *The Works of the Rev. Hugh Binning, M.A.,* ed. M. Leishman (reprint, Ligonier, Pa.: Soli Deo Gloria, 1992), 253–55; Thomas Brooks, *The Works of Thomas Brooks* (reprint, Edinburgh: Banner of Truth Trust, 2001), 4:419–20; Anthony Burgess, *Spiritual Refining: or A Treatise of Grace and Assurance* (London: A Miller for Thomas Underhill, 1652), 237–43; Stephen Charnock, *The Complete Works of Stephen Charnock* (Edinburgh: James Nichol, 1865), 3:90; George Downame, *A Treatise of Ivstification* (London: Felix Kyngston for Nicolas Bourne, 1633), 239–42; John Flavel, *The Works of John Flavel* (Edinburgh: Banner of Truth Trust, 1997), 6:197–99; Thomas Goodwin, *The Works of Thomas Goodwin* (reprint, Grand Rapids: Reformation Heritage Books, 2006), 1:83–102; William Gouge, *A Gvide to Goe to God: or, An explanation of the perfect Patterne of Prayer, The Lords Prayer,* 2nd ed. (London: G.M. for Edward Brewster, 1636), 10–21; Ezekiel Hopkins, *The Works of Ezekiel Hopkins,* ed. Charles W. Quick (reprint, Morgan, Pa.: Soli Deo Gloria, 1997), 2:120–21, 569–76; 3:198–99; Edward Leigh, *A Treatise of Divinity* (London, 1646), 510–11; John Owen, *The Works of John Owen,* ed. William H. Goold (reprint, London: Banner of Truth Trust, 1966), 2:207–22; 4:265–70; 23:255–76.

Thomas Manton, Stephen Marshall, Richard Sibbes, John Tennent, and John Waite, wrote one or more sermons on adoption.[18]

So significant was the Puritan emphasis on adoption that the Westminster Divines were the first to include a separate chapter on the subject of adoption in a confessional statement: the Westminster Confession of Faith (chapter XII). The Larger Cate-

---

18. Jeremiah Burroughs, *The Saints' Happiness, Delivered in Divers Lectures on the Beatitudes* (reprint, Beaver Falls, Pa.: Soli Deo Gloria, 1988), 193–202; Thomas Cole, *A Discourse of Christian Religion, in Sundry Points... Christ the Foundation of our Adoption, from Gal. 4. 5* (London: for Will. Marshall, 1698); Roger Drake, "The Believer's Dignity and Duty Laid Open, in the High Birth wherewith he is Privileged, and the Honourable Employment to which he is Called," in *Puritan Sermons 1659–1689: Being the Morning Exercises at Cripplegate, St. Giles in the Fields, and in Southwark by Seventy-five Ministers of the Gospel in or near London* (reprint, Wheaton, Ill.: Richard Owen Roberts, 1981), 5:328–44; Thomas Hooker, *The Christian's Tvvo Chief Lessons* (reprint, Ames, Iowa: International Outreach, 2002), 159–73; Thomas Manton, *The Complete Works of Thomas Manton, D.D.* (London: James Nisbet, 1870), 1:33–57; 10:116–21; 12:111–39; Stephen Marshall, *The Works of Mr Stephen Marshall, The First Part, [section 2:] The High Priviledge of Beleevers. They are the Sons of God* (London: Peter and Edward Cole, 1661); Richard Sibbes, *Works of Richard Sibbes* (Edinburgh: Banner of Truth Trust, 2001), 4:129–49; John Tennent, "The Nature of Adoption," in *Salvation in Full Color: Twenty Sermons by Great Awakening Preachers*, ed. Richard Owen Roberts (Wheaton, Ill.: International Awakening Press, 1994), 233–50; John Waite, *Of the Creatures Liberation from the Bondage of Corruption, Wherein is Discussed... [section V]: And lastly is discussed that glorious libertie of the sonnes of God into which the creature is to be reduced* (York: Tho: Broad, 1650).

chism (Q. 74) and the Shorter Catechism (Q. 34) also
addressed it, as have numerous commentators of the
Westminster standards ever since.[19] Most important,

---

19. For example, for the Westminster Confession, see Francis
R. Beattie, *The Presbyterian Standards: An Exposition of the
Westminster Confession of Faith and Catechisms* (Richmond,
Va.: Presbyterian Committee of Publication, 1896); 212–16;
David Dickson, *Truth's Victory over Error* (reprint, Edinburgh:
Banner of Truth, 2007), 76–77; A. A. Hodge, *The Westminster
Confession: A Commentary* (reprint, Edinburgh: Banner of
Truth Trust, 2002), 191–93; Joseph A. Pipa, *The Westminster
Confession of Faith Study Book* (Ross-shire, U.K.: Christian
Focus Publications, 2005); Robert Shaw, *The Reformed Faith:
An Exposition of the Westminster Confession of Faith* (reprint,
Inverness: Christian Focus, 1974), 137–41; for the Larger
Catechism, see Thomas Ridgley, *Commentary on the Larger
Catechism* (reprint, Edmonton: Still Waters Revival Books, 1993),
2:131–37; Johannes G. Vos, *The Westminster Larger Catechism:
A Commentary* (Phillipsburg: P & R Publishing, 2002), 164–
66; and for the Shorter Catechism, see Thomas Boston, "An
Illustration of the Doctrines of the Christian Religion," in *The
Complete Works of the Late Rev. Thomas Boston, Ettrick* (reprint,
Stoke-on-Trent, UK: Tentmaker Publications, 2002), 1:612–53;
John Brown (of Haddington), *An Essay towards an easy, plain,
practical, and extensive Explication of the Assembly's Shorter
Catechism* (New York: Robert Carter & Brothers, 1849), 162–65;
James Fisher, *The Assembly's Shorter Catechism Explained, by
way of Question and Answer* (reprint, Lewes, East Sussex: Berith
Publications, 1998), 184–87; John Flavel, "An Exposition of the
Assembly's Catechism," in *The Works of John Flavel* (reprint,
Edinburgh: Banner of Truth Trust, 1997), 6:197–99; Matthew
Henry, "A Scripture Catechism, in the Method of the Assembly's,"
in *The Complete Works of the Rev. Matthew Henry* (reprint,
Grand Rapids: Baker, 1979), 2:209–10; Thomas Vincent, *The
Shorter Catechism of the Westminster Assembly Explained and
Proved from Scripture* (reprint, Edinburgh: Banner of Truth
Trust, 1980), 96–97; Watson, *Body of Divinity*, 155–60. For

some Puritans wrote entire treatises on adoption, including:

- John Crabb, *A Testimony concerning the VVorks of the Living God. Shewing how the mysteries of his workings hath worked many wayes in and amongst mankind. Or, The knowledge of God revealed, which shews the way from the bondage of darkness into the liberty of the Sons of God.*

- Simon Ford, *The Spirit of Bondage and Adoption: Largely and Practically handled, with reference to the way and manner of working both those Effects; and the proper Cases of Conscience belonging to them both.*

- M.G., *The Glorious Excellencie of the Spirit of Adoption.*

- Thomas Granger, *A Looking-Glasse for Christians. Or, The Comfortable Doctrine of Adoption.*

- Cotton Mather, *The Sealed Servants of our God, Appearing with Two Witnesses, to produce a Well-Established Assurance of their being the Children of the Lord Almighty or, the Witness of the Holy Spirit, with the Spirit of the Beleever, to his Adoption of God; briefly and plainly Described.*

- Samuel Petto, *The Voice of the Spirit. Or, An essay towards a discoverie of the witnessings of the Spirit.*

- Samuel Willard, *The Child's Portion: Or the*

---

additional confessional statements that address adoption, see Trumper, "An Historical Study of the Doctrine of Adoption in the Calvinistic Tradition," 5–10.

unseen Glory of the Children of God, Asserted,
and proved: Together with several other Ser-
mons Occasionally Preached. [20]

Sadly, none of these books have been reprinted,
which, in part, serves to promote the misrepresenta-
tion that the Puritans rarely addressed this subject.

Then, too, Scottish and Dutch divines of Puritan persuasion also wrote at length on adoption; for
example, John Forbes, a Church of Scotland minister
who spent most of his pastoral years in the Nether-
lands, wrote, *A Letter for resolving this Question:*
How a Christian man may discerne the testimonie
of Gods spirit, from the testimonie of his owne spirit,
in witnessing his Adoption.[21] Thomas Boston devoted
forty pages to the subject of adoption; Wilhelmus à
Brakel, twenty-five pages.[22] Even Anglican bishops
wrote on the subject; for example, George Bull (1634–
1710), bishop of St. David's, who, though Arminian in

20. Crabb (London: John Gain, 1682); Ford (London: T.
Maxey, for Sa. Gellibrand, 1655); M.G. (London: Jane Coe, for
Henry Overton, 1645); Granger (London: William Iones, 1620);
Mather (Boston: Daniel Henchman, 1727); Petto (London:
Livewell Chapman, 1654); Willard (Boston: Samuel Green, to be
sold by Samuel Phillips, 1684).

21. Middelburg: Richard Schilders, 1616.

22. *The Complete Works of the Late Rev. Thomas Boston,*
Ettrick, ed. Samuel M'Millan (reprint, Wheaton, Ill.: Richard
Owen Roberts, 1980, 1:612–53, 2:15–27); Wilhelmus à Brakel,
The Christian's Reasonable Service, trans. Bartel Elshout, ed.
Joel R. Beeke (Grand Rapids: Reformation Heritage Books, 1999),
2:415–38; 3:486–87.

soteriology had some Puritan sympathies, wrote, *A Discourse Concerning the Spirit of God in the Faithful; how, and in what Manner it doth bear Witness with their Spirits, that they are the Children of God; and what Degree of Hope or Persuasion concerning their Adoption, this Witness of the Spirit doth ordinarily produce in the Faithful.*[23] It is surprising that the book is not very different in content from the Puritan treatises on adoption, except for a lack of emphasis on the wonder of adoption and a downplaying of the Spirit's direct witness to the soul.

The Puritan bibliographical materials recorded in this introduction amount to more than 1,200 pages of writing on the doctrine of spiritual adoption.[24] As far as I know, no one to date has recognized the significant amount of work done by the Puritans on this subject, nor has anyone ever done a study on it. When one considers that the Puritans regarded adoption to be the climax of the *ordo salutis,* and when one considers how extensively Puritan theology has been studied, it is astonishing that this subject has never been examined before. This little book only begins to redress this neglect by letting the Puritans speak for themselves, for the most part; perhaps the foot-

---

23. Reprint, Boston: sold by Thomas Fleet, 1740.

24. This number does not include material that could be included from Puritan commentaries and additional sermons that treat the main texts on adoption, nor additional commentaries on the Westminster standards.

notes will stimulate others to pick up where I have left off. Throughout, I show how Puritanism recognized adoption's far-reaching, transforming power and comfort for the sons and daughters of God.

CHAPTER TWO

———— ◆ ————

The Greatness and Comprehensiveness of Adoption

The Puritans were fond of stressing the transforming power, superlative value, and surprising wonder of adoption. They spoke often of its greatness, excellency, and comprehensiveness.

William Perkins said that a believer should esteem his adoption as God's child as greater than being "the childe or heire of any earthly Prince [since] the sonne of the greatest Potentate may be the childe of wrath: but the child of God by grace, hath Christ Iesus to bee his eldest *brother,* with whom he is *fellow heire* in heaven; hee hath the holy Ghost also for his *comforter,* and the kingdome of heauen for his euerlasting *inheritance.*" Perkins lamented how few people realize this experientially: "At earthly preferments men will stand amazed; but seldome shall you finde a man that is rauished with ioy in this, that hee is the childe of God."[1]

———————

1. *Workes of Perkins,* 3:138 (2nd pagination).

Hugh Binning wrote that to claim to be a son or daughter of God "is a higher word than if a man could deduce his genealogy from an uninterrupted line of a thousand kings and princes. There is more honour, true honour, in it, and more profit too," he concludes, for spiritual adoption "enriches the poorest, and ennobles the basest, inconceivably beyond all the imaginary degrees of men."[2] Jeremiah Burroughs stated it even more strongly by quoting Luther's comment that "if we did but know what this privilege [of adoption] were [*sic*], all the riches of all the kingdoms in the world would be but as filthy dung to us."[3]

"All things are ours by virtue of our adoption," Richard Sibbes wrote, "because we are Christ's and Christ is God's. There is a world of riches in this, to be the sons of God. And what a prerogative is this...that we have boldness to appear before God, to call him Father, to open our necessities, to fetch all things needful, to have the ear of the King of heaven and earth, to be favourites in the court of heaven!"[4]

The greatness of adoption is magnified, as Thomas Manton pointed out, when one considers the contrast between "the person adopting: the great and glorious God" and "the persons who were adopted: miserable sinners" in the light of "the dignity" of the adoption itself. That dignity is so great, Manton

2. *Works of Binning,* 253–54.

3. Burroughs, *The Saints' Happiness,* 194.

4. *Works of Sibbes,* 4:502.

goes on to say, that when it is set beside any other earthly privilege and rightly viewed, we must "blush and hide our faces" because "all the splendid titles which are so ambitiously affected by the world, are but empty shows and gilded vanities, and do much come short of this privilege, both in honour and profit." Moreover, all other titles will perish when we die, but the title of being a son of God will not "cease at the grave's mouth."[5]

Spiritual adoption is the excellency and apex of God's salvation. The Puritans often shared the apostle John's sense of awe when he declared, "Behold, what manner of love the Father hath bestowed upon us, that we should be called the sons of God" (1 John 3:1). What a stupendous wonder adoption is! Wilhelmus à Brakel put it this way: "From being a child of the devil to becoming a child of God, from being a child of wrath to becoming the object of God's favor, from being a child of condemnation to becoming an heir of all the promises and a possessor of all blessings, and to be exalted from the greatest misery to the highest felicity—this is something which exceeds all comprehension and all adoration."[6]

And how comprehensive adoption is! Most Puritans place their treatment of adoption in the ordo salutis between justification and sanctification, following the order set forth by the Westminster

---

5. *Works of Manton*, 12:122.

6. Brakel, *Christian's Reasonable Service*, 2:419.

Divines. Logically, that structure makes considerable sense, given the inevitable ties between justification and adoption, and sanctification and adoption, as we will see shortly. Other Puritans, however, have pointed out that though adoption can at times be viewed as one aspect of salvation, or one part of the ordo salutis, at other times it can be understood best as comprehending all of soteriology. For example, Stephen Marshall writes, "Though sometimes in the holy Scriptures our Sonship is but one of our Priviledges, yet very frequently in the Scripture all the Beleevers do obtain from Christ in this world and the world to come, here and to eternity, all is comprehended in this one, That they are made the Children of God." Marshall goes on to cite several examples: "I know not how often the whol Covenant of Grace is expressed in that word, I wil be their Father, they shal be my children," or consider Ephesians 1:5, he says, where Paul comprehends all of salvation "in this one expression, having predestinated us to the adoption of children."[7]

Clearly, the Puritans ascribed a lofty and comprehensive place to adoption in their soteriology. Recent studies have reaffirmed and even surpassed the Puritans in giving adoption a place of prominence. In his recent, excellent dissertation, "Adoption in Christ,"

---

7. Marshall also uses Romans 8:23 and the beginning of Galatians 4 to buttress Scripture's frequent comprehensive use of adoption (*Works of Stephen Marshall,* 37–38).

David Garner argues that adoption in Scripture is coterminous and nearly synonymous with union with Christ; hence, it should never be placed in the *schema* of the *ordo salutis* as an individual aspect, but ought to be always regarded as an overarching doctrine that embraces the whole of soteriology.[8] In essence, that is Marshall's position as well, though Marshall allows for interpreting certain texts on adoption, such as Romans 8:14–17, as accenting one aspect of the *ordo salutis*. It seems to me that Marshall is more accurate here. The question of whether adoption is one aspect of the *ordo salutis* or comprehensive of its whole is not an "either–or" but a "both–and" proposition, dependent on the particular text being examined.

Robert Peterson throws the net out even wider. He sees adoption as "an overarching way of viewing the Christian faith," arguing that adoption influences most major theological *loci*.[9] That concept is most intriguing, and it is worthy of further study and development.

---

8. Garner, "Adoption in Christ," 229–53.

9. Peterson, "Toward a Systematic Theology of Adoption," *Presbyterion,* 27, no. 2 (Fall 2001): 121.

CHAPTER THREE

———— ◆ ————

Adoption Compared
in the Two Testaments

The Puritans believed that the metaphors of "adoption" and "sons of God" are valid for believers of both testaments, but that only in the New Testament did the transforming power of adoption come to the fore. Herman Witsius, one of the clearest on this point, stresses that believers in the Old Testament era were also regenerated, betrothed to Christ, and adopted to become sons of God. He writes that "believers, at all times, were the children of God. Elihu, who was not of the people of Israel, called God *his Father*." Yet the clarity on the adoption of Old Testament believers compared to New Testament believers varies as much as "the light of the stars before that of the sun."[1]

Witsius goes on to say that believers under the Old Testament were children under the "severity and discipline of tutors, who bound heavy burdens, grievous to be borne, and laid them on their shoulders."

———————

1. Witsius, *The Economy of the Covenants,* 1:447.

Consequently, believers were "obliged to be subject to the weak and beggarly elements of the world, and like children, to be engaged all the day in the trifling ceremonies of the Mosaic institution, which were, in a manner, the play-things of the church." Compared with New Testament believers, they were taught like infants, "without being left to their own choice," and experienced little "familiarity" with their Father. They were not allowed to enter the temple, and they were compelled to live under types and shadows by sacrifices and offerings in the land of Canaan which served as a rather obscure pledge of the heavenly inheritance.[2]

New Testament believers bask in the sunlight of God's superabounding, adopting grace and liberty merited for them by their Elder Brother. Witsius writes, "For after our elder brother, having taken upon him human nature, had visited this lower world, and freely undergone a state of various servitude for us, he brought us into true liberty, John viii. 36. removed the tutors, [and] blotted out the hand-writing of ordinances, which was contrary to us." He now brings us into the Father's "secret counsels," shows us the Father by showing us Himself (John 14:9), and makes us into a royal priesthood (1 Peter 2:9). He calls us "directly to an inheritance of spiritual and heavenly good things, and appoints unto us a kingdom" (cf. Luke 22:29). Believers are now "eminently

---

2. Ibid., 447–48.

and emphatically called *the sons of God*" (1 John 3:2), as Isaiah had prophesied (Isa. 56:4–5), and the Holy Spirit witnesses with their spirits that this is so (Rom. 8:15–16). God consciously becomes their personal Father, and this name "Father" becomes God's new covenant name, representing the family covenant to which He binds Himself on behalf of His children, so that they now have liberty to cry, "Abba, Father" (Gal. 4:6).

Galatians 4:4–7 teaches, Witsius goes on to say, that "*when the fulness of the time was come; namely, that appointed time,* (till which the children were to be under tutors, ver. 2.) *God sent forth his Son to redeem them that were under the law,* setting them free from the use of ceremonies, *and that we might receive the adoption.*" They "receive the adoption" into Christ's kingdom provided for by the testament of Christ's blood. That kingdom consists of the whole world, so that every crumb of bread believers receive, every aspect of creation they observe, and every act of providence carried out testifies of the love of the Father and [is for] their own good. To this spiritual kingdom entered into by adoption belong victory over sin, the bruising of Satan, inestimable riches, peace of soul, joy in the Holy Spirit, and boldness in Christ (Eph. 3:12).[3]

The four major Pauline texts that deal with believers as the sons of God (Eph. 1:4–5; Gal. 4:4–6;

---

3. Ibid., 448–54.

Rom. 8:15–16; Rom. 8:23), have been summarized
as follows: "The Father in love eternally predestinated all Christians to this privilege of adoption. The
Father sent his own Son Jesus Christ into the world
to redeem us from the curse of the broken law so
that we might enjoy this privileged status of adopted
sons. Now that we are in Christ we do not have the
Spirit of bondage but we have the Holy Spirit's assurance that we are God's children and can approach
him with that confidence. The same Holy Spirit who
dwells in us also gives us anticipatory groanings in
our soul for the state of resurrection and glory which
is the goal that God has appointed for us."[4]

---

4. Maurice Roberts, "The Doctrine of Adoption" (unpublished
paper, delivered at Free Reformed Ministers' Conference in
Puslinch, Ontario, 2003), 9.

———— ♦ ————

CHAPTER FOUR

What Adoption Is Not

To analyze more precisely the Puritans' teachings on adoption, it is advantageous to consider first what they thought adoption is not.

Adoption is not regeneration

We are prone to treat regeneration and adoption as synonymous because the regenerated Christian is someone born from above. Adoption, at first glance, seems to be another way of describing the consequences of that new birth. The Puritans assure us, however, that this is not so. These are two distinct blessings, though all who are born again are adopted, and everyone who is adopted is born again.[1]

Regeneration and adoption deal with two different problems. Adoption deals with our status. We are by nature children of wrath and children of the devil; our status is one of alienation and condemnation.

———————

1. Jeremiah Burroughs stresses the wonder and mystery of the gospel that God both regenerates and adopts us by His unspeakable grace (*The Saints' Happiness,* 192).

Because of the sin-removing and heaven-meriting work of Christ, our whole status changes so that we are now called the children of God.

If in adoption we were to receive only the privilege and status of being God's children, something would still be missing. The adopted child retains the nature of his biological parents; he does not assume the nature of the adoptive parents. God, in His amazing grace, not only gives us the status and privileges of being His children by adoption, but He also gives us the Spirit of sonship as a witness to our adoption, which abides within us by Spirit-worked regeneration. The Holy Spirit implants a new nature within us.

Regeneration, then, deals with our nature, those sinful hearts of ours that drink iniquity like water. God changes our sin-loving personalities by the new birth. In other words, after changing our status and adopting us into His family as His sons, God will not allow us to go on behaving like children of the devil. He ensures that we cannot do so; He gives us the nature and likeness to match our sonship by a birth from above. Our title as "a son of God" then becomes intimately related to our own experience. We are not what we once were (1 John 3:9). God has done what no human father and mother can do when they adopt a child — change the personality and the nature of the child they have adopted so that it is like theirs. But God, in regeneration, has allowed His born-again children to become partakers of His own loving, holy nature as their Father in heaven.

In short, the Puritans taught that regeneration and adoption are to be distinguished in several ways. Here is a summary of points made by Thomas Manton and Stephen Charnock:

- Regeneration brings us to close with Christ; adoption causes the Spirit to abide in our hearts.

- Regeneration is the Spirit's renewing; adoption, the Spirit's inhabiting. In regeneration, the Holy Spirit builds a house for Himself; in adoption, He dwells in the house—much like bees that "first make their cells, and then dwell in them."

- Regeneration is not conditioned by faith; adoption is.

- Regeneration enables us to believe unto justification and adoption.

- Regeneration engraves upon us the lineaments of a father; adoption relates us to God as our Father.

- Regeneration makes us God's sons by conveying the principle of new life (1 Pet. 1:23); adoption keeps us God's sons by conferring the power of new life (John 1:12).

- Regeneration makes us partakers of the divine nature; adoption makes us partakers of the divine affections.

- Regeneration affects our nature; adoption, our relationships.[2]

---

2. *Works of Manton,* 12:113–14; *Complete Works of Charnock,* 3:90.

Anthony Burgess explains that maintaining such distinctions as these "keep us from proud presumption on the one hand," for we are dependent on God for both regeneration and adoption, and yet they are "a great incentive to Godlinesse on the other hand," for the adopted child yearns to know his Father better.[3]

Adoption is not justification

Justification is the primary, fundamental blessing of the gospel; it meets our most basic spiritual need—forgiveness and reconciliation with God. We could not be adopted without it. But adoption is a richer blessing, because it brings us from the court room into the family. "Justification is conceived of in terms of law, adoption in terms of love. Justification sees God as a judge, adoption as a father."[4]

Justification and adoption obviously have much in common. The Puritans taught that the status of adoption, like justification, is an act rather than a process. Contrary to Robert Bellarmine and Roman Catholicism, this act is administered by imputation, not infusion.[5] It is punctiliar, not linear. Believers are not progressively adopted, becoming more and more

---

3. Burgess, *Spiritual Refining,* 238.

4. Gordon Cooke, "The Doctrine of Adoption and the Preaching of Jeremiah Burroughs," 23.

5. George Downame, *A Treatise of Ivstification* (London: Felix Kyngston for Nicolas Bourne, 1633), 241–42.

the children of God; adoption is no more subject to degrees than justification is. When sinners believe, they are made full children of God and remain such. Justification declares them to be righteous — in a moment! They go sinful and naked to God and ask Him to forgive their sins, and He replies exceedingly abundantly above all that they could ask or think (Eph. 3:20). In a moment God changes their status forever. They become His children, sons and heirs of God, joint heirs with Christ.

When an attempt is made to pinpoint more precisely the relationship of justification and adoption, three viewpoints surface among the Puritans. The first, represented by Wilhelmus à Brakel, says that since justification includes not only a negative aspect of acquittal from guilt and punishment, but also a positive aspect of the bestowal of the right of eternal life, in which God's children are declared heirs, adoption is best seen as being included in the positive side of justification. Hence, justification includes spiritual sonship.[6] Notwithstanding this position, however, it is interesting to note that Brakel still treats adop-

---

6. This is also the position of the *Sonship* program that originated as a Bible study in New Life Presbyterian Church, Jenkintown, Pennsylvania, under the leadership of Jack Miller. The program seeks to train church members in evangelism. For an evaluation of the program, see Chad Van Dixhoorn ("The *Sonship* Program, for Revival: A Summary and Critique," *Westminster Theological Journal* 61 [1999]: 227–46). Van Dixhoorn asserts that "by establishing continuous surprising revival as the standard of piety for the church, *Sonship* not only causes the individual

tion as a separate chapter in his exposition of the *ordo salutis*. Unfortunately, subsequent writers that upheld this position often subsumed adoption in the same chapter as justification, almost relegating it to a footnote.

The second position, represented by Thomas Ridgley, a moderate Calvinist best known for his exposition of the Westminster Larger Catechism, is that adoption is included in justification from one perspective but not from another. Ridgley maintains that adoption can be reckoned as a branch of justification in some respects and a branch of sanctification in other respects. He writes, "If justification be explained as denoting an immanent act in God, whereby the elect are considered, in the covenant between the Father and the Son, as in Christ their federal head; they are then considered as the adopted children of God in Christ. Accordingly, when described as chosen in Christ unto eternal life, they are said to be 'predestinated unto the adoption of children.'" Both justification and adoption, Ridgley adds, are received by faith. On the other hand, if adoption is viewed from the perspective of the child of God's being made meet for his heavenly inheritance, which includes "being endowed with the temper and disposition of his children, consisting in humility, heavenly-mindedness, love to him, dependence upon

Christian to look for the extraordinary, but forces the corporate church to do the same" (ibid., 245).

him, a zeal for his glory, a likeness to Christ, a having in some measure the same mind in us which was in him, it in this respect agrees with sanctification."[7]

Third, the majority of the Puritans support the position of the Westminster Assembly, stressing that justification and adoption, though intimately related, are two distinct privileges and ought to be handled separately in theology. For example, in expounding the Shorter Catechism, Samuel Willard emphasizes that the Bible clearly distinguishes justification and adoption in Romans 8:14ff., Ephesians 1:5, and elsewhere. Scripture makes plain that it is one thing to be judged righteous and another to be placed among God's children; "one thing to have God accept us as a Judge, another to do so as a Father," with all the love and care that that involves. Justification involves a *legal* relationship; adoption, a *personal* relationship. Then, too, though both justification and adoption involve a title of inheritance, they receive that title on different grounds. Willard asserts that "if *Adam* had persisted in his Integrity, he had enjoyed this title in way of Justification, but not of Adoption; for it has its rooting in the first Covenant, whereas this, entirely belongs to, and hath its rise from the new Covenant." Finally, Willard points out that adoption involves privileges that do not depend on justification. For example, if Adam had remained standing, he would have been justified, but not adopted in

---

7. Ridgley, *Commentary on the Larger Catechism,* 136–37.

the sense that new covenant believers are now, "for doubtless, the state of God's Children under the new Covenant, is better than that of *Adam* and his posterity, would have been under the first, had he kept his uprightness."[8]

These three positions, practically speaking, are not far removed from one another. Theologically, however, the second, and especially the third, are prone to accent adoption more biblically, though all three can be adapted to fit Sinclair Ferguson's apt summary: "Undoubtedly the New Testament never separates justification and adoption, but neither does it confuse them. In human terms it is quite possible to imagine a man being justified without the remotest thought of his being adopted. The fact that a judge pronounces the verdict of 'not guilty' does not commit him to take the accused to his home and allow him all the privileges of his son!"[9]

Though both justification and adoption are forensic concepts — the former derived from the realm of criminal law and the latter from family law — their practical outworkings differ substantially. Justification in abstraction from adoption leaves us with a rather bare, legal concept — though, of course, the privilege of having our sins forgiven and being made

---

8. Willard, *A Compleat Body of Divinity,* 482–83.

9. Sinclair B. Ferguson, *Know Your Christian Life: A Theological Introduction* (Downers Grove, Ill: InterVarsity Press, 1981), 82.

acceptable to God must never be underestimated. But adoption enlarges our understanding of what it means to be acceptable to God. We are acceptable not simply as moral agents, but as the image-bearers of our Father who are being subjectively conformed to Christ. We are acceptable as sons of God who have the privilege of calling God our Father and bear the responsibility of serving Him as His children.

Subjectively, of course, believers grow in the knowledge of their adoption, as is considered in more detail below.[10] Thus, the Puritans taught that adoption in its objective dimension, related to the believer's state and to justification, is instantaneous and complete; in its subjective dimension, related to the believer's condition and to sanctification, there is a growing awareness of its privileges, responsibilities, and applications.

Adoption is not sanctification

Thomas Brooks asserts that sanctification is simply a living out of one's adoption and sonship (John 1:12; Rom. 8:17). It is a cultivating of family characteristics. He writes, "If thou art a holy person, then of a child of wrath thou art become a child of God, a child of love; and of an heir of hell thou art become an heir of heaven; and of a slave, thou art become a son."[11]

The Puritans would resonate well with J. I. Packer's

---

10. See the section on how adoption is realized experientially.

11. *Works of Thomas Brooks,* 4:419.

assertion that sanctification is "simply a consistent living out of our filial relationship with God, into which the gospel brings us. It is just a matter of the child of God being true to type, true to his Father, to his Saviour, and to himself. It is the expressing of one's adoption in one's life. It is a matter of being a good son, as distinct from a prodigal or black sheep in the royal family."[12]

Through sanctification the believer is brought into a fuller experiential awareness of his adoption. He learns to grasp more fully what adoption is, and he learns to live out of its wonders. The Holy Spirit enables him to break off more and more all lingering traits and ties of the old family life, and out of love to our Father to submit willingly to the disciplines and authority that He exercises for the good of His children.

By the Spirit's grace, our lives then become increasingly regulated by His Word and will. Though there will be setbacks and failings, we will grow in righteousness and true holiness, thereby reflecting the character of our heavenly Father. We become increasingly conformed to the likeness of the family Prototype, His eternal Son.

In sum, sanctification prepares us for the full and consummate enjoyment of the inheritance to which adoption entitles: joint heirship with Christ.

---

12. Packer, *Knowing God,* 201.

———— ◆ ————

CHAPTER FIVE

The Westminster Assembly's Definitions of Adoption

The Westminster Assembly, which included scores of Puritans, offers three formal definitions of adoption—a basic definition in the Shorter Catechism (hereafter SC), an intermediate definition in the Larger Catechism (hereafter LC), and a more comprehensive definition in the Confession of Faith (hereafter WCF):

> *Shorter Catechism, Q. 34:* Adoption is an act of God's free grace, whereby we are received into the number, and have a right to all the privileges, of the sons of God.

> *Larger Catechism, Q. 74:* Adoption is an act of the free grace of God, in and for His only Son Jesus Christ, whereby all those that are justified are received into the number of His children, have His name put upon them, the Spirit of His Son given to them, are under His fatherly care and dispensations, admitted to all the liberties and privileges of the sons of God, made heirs of all the promises, and fellow heirs with Christ in glory.

Confession of Faith, Chap. XII: All those that are justified, God vouchsafeth, in and for His only Son Jesus Christ, to make partakers of the grace of adoption, by which they are taken into the number, and enjoy the liberties and privileges of the children of God, have His name put upon them, receive the spirit of adoption, have access to the throne of grace with boldness, are enabled to cry, Abba, Father, are pitied, protected, provided for, and chastened by Him as by a Father: yet never cast off, but sealed to the day of redemption; and inherit the promises, as heirs of everlasting salvation.[1]

Several significant points may be made relative to the Westminster Assembly's work on adoption:

First, how intriguing it is that the Westminster Divines, often accused of being too harsh and rigid in their theology, provided the Christian church's first confessional chapter and formal articles on adoption — one of the most tender doctrines of the Christian faith! Why the assembly decided to allot adoption a separate *locus* is not clear. Both the published and unpublished minutes of the Westminster Assembly tell us no more than the basic dates and facts that it happened.[2] Perhaps the Divines were motivated by a growing awareness of the scriptur-

---

1. *Reformed Confessions Harmonized,* ed. Joel R. Beeke and Sinclair B. Ferguson (Grand Rapids: Baker, 1999), 107.

2. See Trumper, "An Historical Study of the Doctrine of Adoption in the Calvinistic Tradition," 227–29, for a detailed study of Westminster's minutes relative to adoption.

alness and importance of adoption both doctrinally and experientially as it relates to justification, sanctification, assurance of faith, perseverance, and other ancillary doctrines.

Second, there are good reasons for the Westminster Divines' brevity in treating adoption, including the lack of treatment in former confessions, the lack of dissent or heresy that needed to be addressed, and the overlap of material with the chapters on assurance and perseverance. All of these factors assist the Divines to expound a large doctrine with remarkably succinct brevity.[3] We should not be deceived by its size.

It may appear like a thin filling in a thick sandwich in the way it is placed between the doctrines of justification and sanctification, but it is a topic of enormous depth and breadth and is highly significant because of its implications for a proper understanding of the gospel of Christ.

Third, the Westminster Divines were concerned to apply predestination soteriologically, as is evident in WCF III:vi, where the first reference to adoption is made in conjunction with predestination: "They who are elected, being fallen in Adam, are redeemed by Christ, are effectually called unto faith in Christ by His Spirit working in due season, are justified, *adopted*, sanctified, and kept by His power, through

---

3. Chad Van Dixhoorn, "The *Sonship* Program, for Revival: A Summary and Critique," *Westminster Theological Journal* 61 (1999): 235–36.

faith, unto salvation. Neither are there any other
redeemed by Christ, effectually called, justified,
adopted, sanctified, and saved, but the elect only"
(emphasis added). Later, the assembly stressed that
adoption originates as "an act of the free grace of
God" (LC 74; cf. SC 34 and WCF III:v), and involves
being "taken" (WCF XII) or "received into the number" of the elect (SC 34; LC 74). Tim Trumper rightly
concludes that "as the Westminster commissioners
were as concerned as Calvin to apply predestination
soteriologically, there is little purpose in driving a
wedge between Calvin and the later Calvinists" on
this issue, as is often done.[4]

Fourth, union with Christ is inseparable from
adoption. The sonship we receive is Christ's in the
first place. Adoption transpires "in and for His Son
Jesus Christ," so that the adopted "have His name
put upon them, the Spirit of His Son given to them"
(LC 74; WCF XII). Justification, adoption, and sanctification all flow from union with Christ (LC 69).
Contrary to what some scholars have suggested, the
Westminster Divines were as concerned as Calvin
to maintain that "to be adopted is to be united with
Christ in his Sonship."[5]

Fifth, the Westminster Divines harmonized the
forensic and familial elements of adoption. They

---

4. Trumper, "An Historical Study of the Doctrine of Adoption
in the Calvinistic Tradition," 231.

5. Ibid., 232.

spoke of both the judicial pronouncement of adoption (LC 74; WCF VIII:v, XII) and the adoptive experience of sonship, referred to as the "liberties and privileges" of adoption (LC 74; WCF XII). This union is also evident in the chapter on justification, where forensic and familial aspects are united in the statement that though the justified "can never fall from the state of justification, yet they may, by their sins, fall under God's *fatherly* displeasure" (WCF XI:v, emphasis added). Adoption, therefore, is not exhausted by its forensic aspects; rather, the forensic aspects imply an ensuing familial life of sonship that manifests itself in the visible church, which is described as "the house and family of God" (WCF XXV:ii).[6]

Finally, the Westminster Divines emphasize that adoption is an act of free grace (SC 34, LC 74, WCF XII). In adoption, the unlovable sinner is freely loved by God and taken into the divine family. "He doth not Adopt us, because we were lovely, but that wee might be so," says Samuel Willard. "God saw as much beauty in others as in us, and that was none at all. And hence, that yet he should adopt us, is a demonstration of his unconceivable Grace."[7] Thomas Watson puts it this way: "Adoption is a mercy spun out of the bowels of free grace; all by nature are strangers, therefore have no right to sonship, only

---

6. Ibid., 234–36.

7. Willard, *A Compleat Body of Divinity*, 486.

God is pleased to adopt one, and not another, to make one a vessel of glory, another a vessel of wrath. The adopted heir may cry out, 'Lord, how is it, that thou wilt show thyself to me, and not unto the world?'"[8]

---

8. Watson, *A Body of Practical Divinity*, 155.

CHAPTER SIX

———— ♦ ————

The Transforming Power of Adoption

Believers are not sons of God by nature. We lost the status and privileges of God's image-bearers in our tragic fall in Paradise. Adoption is only made possible when God's gracious choice brings us into all the privileges and blessings of being in His family as His children and establishing a filial relationship with us so that we respond with childlike feelings of love, obedience, hope, and dependence towards God, and we look up to Him for our every need, for this life and a better, as a child looks to his or her father.[1]

When we are born again, God delivers us from Satan's enslaving family and, by His astounding grace, transfers us to the Father's sonship. He calls us sons; we are adopted into His family, transferred "from a state of sin and misery" to "a state of excellency [and] dignity," writes Watson. "It were much

---

1. *Works of Manton,* 12:114–16; Maurice Roberts, "The Doctrine of Adoption," 1–2.

for God to take a clod of dust and make it a star; it is more for God to take a piece of clay and sin and adopt it for his heir."[2]

Adoption in the time of the apostle John usually took place in adolescence or adulthood, not infancy. Under Roman law, adoption was a legal act by which a man chose someone outside of the family to be an heir to his inheritance. Likewise, believers become children of God through the gracious act of God the Father, who chooses them to be His heirs and joint heirs with Christ.

William Ames says there are four differences between human and divine adoption:

- Human adoption relates to a person, who, as a stranger, has no right to the inheritance except through adoption. But believers, though by natural birth they have no right to the inheritance of life, are given it because of rebirth, faith, and justification.

- Human adoption is only an outward designation and bestowal of external things. But divine adoption is so real a relationship that it is based on an inward action and the communications of a new inner life.

- Human adoption was introduced when there were no, or too few, natural sons. But divine adoption is not from any want but from abundant goodness, whereby a likeness of a natural son and mystical union is given to the adopted sons.

---

2. Watson, *A Body of Practical Divinity*, 156.

- The human adoption is ordained so that the son may succeed the father in the inheritance. But divine adoption is not ordained for succession, but for participation in the inheritance assigned. Both the Father and his first-begotten Son live forever and this admits no succession.[3]

There are differences, too, between human and divine adoption with regard to what Samuel Willard calls "grounds or reasons." He lists these: (1) Unlike God, who lives forever, people must leave their estates behind them when they die, and if they have no heir, they eventually will be forgotten. (2) Unlike God, people often fail to have an heir and feel forced to make one. (3) Unlike God's adopted people, who participate in their inheritance from the moment they are made joint heirs with God, the adopted in natural life must wait for the death of their adopters before they can receive their inheritance. (4) Unlike God, whose decrees are unalterable, people can change their heirs while they live. (5) Unlike God, who chooses His adopted children for no reasons seen in them, people choose their heirs for reasons that relate to the heirs. (6) Unlike God, who infuses His adopted children with sanctifying qualities, people cannot change the inner core of their heirs.[4]

---

3. Ames, *The Marrow of Theology*, 165–67.

4. Willard, *A Compleat Body of Divinity*, 483–84. Cf. Cole, *Christ the Foundation of Our Adoption*, 343–45; Ridgley, *Commentary on the Larger Catechism*, 2:132–33; *Works of Bates*, 4:300–301; Brendan Byrne, 'Sons of God'—'Seed of Abraham': A

Then, too, how astonishing it is that, unlike people's heirs who don't share their estates with their friends, we as God's adopted children share the same privileges that belong to God's only-begotten Son! The Puritans reveled in what Christ prays in John 17:23: "[Thou] hast loved them, as thou hast loved me."[5] This love is the essence of God's fatherhood. It shows us how far God is willing to go to reconcile us to Himself.

How great is the love the Father has lavished on us that we should be called children of God (1 John 3:1)—we who deserve His judgment, dethroned Him from our lives, spurned His love, and defied His laws. We never deserve God's love, yet He graciously lavishes love on us in Christ. Here, surely, is the great assurance of the child of God, that God the Father loved him when he was bound for hell. God loved the sinner who had no thought of God in his heart, and He adopted him. How wonderful is the assurance of the Father's words: "I have loved thee with an everlasting love" (Jer. 31:3).

Love and communion with God lie at the heart of adoption, according to John Owen. Owen listed five elements of adoption, which Sinclair Ferguson sum-

---

Study of the Idea of the Sonship of God of All Christians in Paul Against the Jewish Background (Rome: Biblical Institute, 1979).

5. Anthony Burgess, *CXLV Expository Sermons Upon the whole 17th Chapter of the Gospel According to John* (London: Abraham Miller for Thomas Underhill, 1656), 641–48.

marizes as follows: "(1) that the person first belongs to another family; (2) that there is a family to which he has no right to belong; (3) that there is an authoritative legal translation from one family to another; (4) that the adopted person is freed from all the legal obligations of the family from which he came; and (5) that by virtue of his translation he is invested with all the rights, privileges, and advantages of the new family."[6]

The Puritans emphasize that all the members of the Trinity are involved in our adoption. Stephen Marshall summarizes it this way: Adoption is the gracious act of God the Father whereby He chooses us, calls us to Himself, and gives us the privileges and blessings of being His children. God the Son earned those blessings for us through His propitiatory death and sacrifice, by which we become children of God (1 John 4:10), and applies them to us as Elder Brother. And the Holy Spirit changes us from children of wrath, which we are by nature, into children of God by means of regeneration; unites us to Christ; works in us a "suitable disposition" towards God and Christ; and seals our sonship as the Spirit of adoption, witnessing with our spirits that we are the sons of God. In that witnessing, the Spirit shows us God's work of grace in our hearts and lives, and also "car-

---

6. Ferguson, *John Owen on the Christian Life,* 90–91; cf. *Works of Owen,* 2:207ff.

ries our hearts to God, and testifies to the Soul that God is [our] Father."[7]

This adopted relationship with God contains several properties. John Flavel summarizes them: "It is a costly relation (Gal. 4:4), a high and honourable relation (1 John 3:1), a free relation on God's part (Eph. 1:4–5), and a permanent relation (John 8:35)."[8] In short, God's children are loved, ruled, and guided by their heavenly Father—forever!

---

7. *Works of Marshall*, 43–48.

8. *Works of Flavel*, 6:198. Boston expands on these same properties (*Works of Boston*, 2:626–27), as does Drake (*Puritan Sermons*, 5:332–33).

♦

CHAPTER SEVEN

Pastoral Advice in Promoting Adoption

As pastors, the Puritans distinguished people in four ways with regard to adoption.

Visible adoption

First, some are visibly adopted into God's church family but lack its experiential power. Their adoption, says Thomas Shepard, is "external, whereby the Lord takes a people by outward covenant and dispensation to be his sons, and thus all the Jews were God's 'first born,' (Ex. iv. 22,) and unto them did 'belong the adoption,' (Rom. ix. 4, 5;) and hence their children were accounted 'sons' as well as saints, and 'holy,' (1 Cor. vii. 14; Ezek. xvi. 20, 21;) but many fall from this adoption, as the Jews did."[1]

Today, this visible adoption applies to the New

---

1. Shepard, *The Sincere Convert and the Sound Believer*, 251. Cf. Burgess, *Spiritual Refining*, 238–39; Drake, *Puritan Sermons*, 5:329–30; Watson, *A Body of Practical Divinity*, 155.

Testament church. Many have professed the gospel as members of the church but do not know the gospel's power. Not being born again, they do not possess the Spirit of adoption. That fault is not the gospel's but their own. Manton writes, "They are strangers to the grace of the covenant under which they live, by their own negligence and folly." Manna is around their tents, Manton continues, but they would rather starve than gather it. "The Spirit is ready, but they are lazy," he concludes.[2]

Such people are "under a visible administration of the covenant of grace." Christ often gives them "common gifts which he giveth not to the heathen world: knowledge of the mysteries of godliness; abilities of utterance and speech about spiritual and heavenly things; some affection also to them, called 'tasting of the good word, the heavenly gift, and the powers of the world to come,' Heb. vi." Despite having these common gifts of superficial Christianity, they lack "the real Christianity with special graces."[3]

Ministers must warn such people of the danger of remaining members of Satan's family inwardly while they appear to be members of God's family. They must plead with sinners to repent and believe in Christ and trust God's mercy for adoption. Roger

---

2. *Works of Manton,* 12:116.
3. Ibid.

Drake says, "Art thou an alien? O never rest till thou get into a [saving] state of sonship."[4]

Under the Spirit of bondage

Second, some professing members of the church are under "the Spirit of bondage," that is, those who are under the Holy Spirit's power to convict of sin but do not as yet have liberty in Christ. Some Puritans — though by no means all — understand this to mean what is at times called "a preparatory work of grace." Simon Ford devotes 180 pages to describing this convicting work of the Spirit.[5] Ezekiel Hopkins lays out the essence of this approach more succinctly; his key thoughts form an apt summary:

(1) The preparatory work of conversion is usually carried on in the soul by legal fears and terrors.

(2) This legal fear is slavish, and engenders bondage.

(3) This slavish fear is wrought in the soul by the Spirit of God, though it be slavish.

(4) When the soul is prepared for the work of grace by the work of conviction, when it is prepared for comfort by the work of humiliation, the same Spirit, that was before a Spirit of bondage, becomes now a Spirit of adoption.

(5) To whom the Spirit hath once been a Spirit of adoption, it never more becomes to them a Spirit of bondage and fear.

---

4. Drake, *Puritan Sermons*, 5:340.
5. Ford, *The Spirit of Bondage and Adoption*, 1–180.

(6) A reverential, filial fear of God, may and ought
to possess our souls, while the Spirit of God, who
is a spirit of adoption, is, by the clearest evidences,
actually witnessing our sonship to us.[6]

Pastorally, the Puritans advised those who were
under the Spirit of bondage of their danger, their invitation, and their encouragement. Their danger is that
they will perish if they do not take refuge in Christ
with penitent faith and come to know the Spirit of
adoption. Their invitation is to come to Christ immediately, confessing their sins—including the sin of
lacking childlike fear. They must be advised to ask
the Spirit to drive them out of their self-confidence
and cause them to storm the mercy seat. And their
encouragement is, according to Simon Ford, that
God will not keep His elect indefinitely in bondage
for several reasons: religion would become uncom-
fortable and unappealing, people would faint under
their burden of sin, and they would develop hard
thoughts of God. God will lead those under bondage
into liberty to show that one does not serve Him in
vain; He wants to wean His own from this world, and
He wants to commune often with them.[7]

Weak sense of sonship
Third, some sincere children of God have, at best,
a weak sense of their own sonship. Objectively, all

---

6. *Works of Hopkins*, 2:569–74.

7. Ford, *The Spirit of Bondage and Adoption*, 212–16.

God's children are equally sons with God, as we have seen. But, as Manton says, "All God's children have the spirit of adoption in the effects, though not in the sense and feeling of it. They have the spirit of comfort, though not the comfort of it.... There is a child-like inclination and impression left upon them, though they know it not, [and] own it not." Christ had the Spirit without measure, but Christians, though having the whole Spirit, enjoy Him and His work in different degrees. Christians are not all of the same size and growth. Subjectively, some do not "have the spirit of adoption at so full a rate as others have; neither so pure and fervent a love to God; nor such a respectful obedience and submission to him; nor such an holy confidence and boldness, becoming that great happiness which they are called unto, who have the right and hope of the blessed inheritance; and so not so much of that son-like disposition, which the Spirit worketh by revealing the love and mercy of God, contained in the gospel, in the hearts of his people." Manton concludes, "Some do more improve their privileges than others do; now they cannot rationally expect the best and richest fruits of this gift, and to be enabled and enlarged by the Spirit, who do not give such ready entertainment and obedience to his motions, as the more serious and fruitful Christian doth."[8]

Manton then explains the difference between

---

8. *Works of Manton,* 12:116–17.

these people who have a weak sense of sonship and those who are still under the Spirit of bondage. These people have a childlike inclination to God, though they lack childlike familiarity and boldness. They have a childlike reverence for God as Father (1 Peter 1:17), though they lack a childlike confidence in Him as their Father. They have a childlike dependence on God's general offers of grace, but they are not persuaded of the sincerity of their particular claim. They have a childlike love to God, though they lack assurance of His paternal love to them. They possess the childlike adherence of faith without the mature, full assurance of faith. They experience, at times, both childlike groans (Rom. 8:26) and childlike comforts (1 Peter 1:8). And their heart is drawn out to heavenly truths, though they often cannot claim such truths as their own. Unlike those under the Spirit of bondage who seek God out of a mercenary spirit, these seek Him from a childlike spirit.[9]

Manton gives four counsels to assist the weak in faith in being able to call God their Father:

First, "disclaim when you cannot apply." If you cannot say "Father," plead on your "fatherless" condition, using such texts as Hosea 14:3: "In thee the fatherless find mercy."

Second, "own God in the humbling way." Come to the Father like the prodigal son, confessing your unworthiness, or like Paul, as the chief of sinners.

---

9. Ibid., 1:34–36; 12:117–18.

Come to Him as your Father-Creator if you cannot come to Him as your Father-Savior.

Third, "call him Father in wish." If you cannot call Him Father with directness, do it with desire. "Let us pray ourselves into this relation, and groan after it, that we may have a clearer sense that God is our Father in Christ," he counsels.

Fourth, make "use of Christ Jesus." Since Christ's name means so much in heaven, "if you cannot come to God as your Father, come to him as the God and Father of our Lord Jesus Christ (Eph. 3:14). Let Christ bring you into God's presence. He is willing to change relations with us. Take him along with you in your arms. Go to God in Christ's name: 'Whatsoever you ask in my name, shall be given to you.'"[10]

Strong sense of sonship

Finally, many believers experience the joy of knowing that they are sons and daughters of God. That knowledge is grounded in objective truth — ultimately, in God's election. God's will is the foundation in this building: He "predestinated us unto the adoption of children...according to the good pleasure of his will" (Eph. 1:5). Election is executed by means of Christ's bloody atonement: Christ was "made of a woman, made under the law,...that we might receive the adoption of sons" (Gal. 4:4–5). Christ purchased the

---

10. Ibid., 1:36, 50–51; cf. Ford, *The Spirit of Bondage and Adoption,* 200, and Petto, *The Voice of the Spirit,* 56–62.

adoption of His brothers and sisters by His obedience and satisfaction. He also sends out His ministers, as Boston says, "to proclaim the offer of adoption unto them, that whosoever of them will leave their father's house and people [i.e., Satan and the unsaved] shall be adopted into the family of heaven." Satan rages against this message, but "unto the elect among them God sends his Spirit, which opens their ears, awakens their conscience, and rouses them so, that they can no longer" live without a Savior.[11] The Spirit then applies Christ's satisfying atonement in regeneration, which immediately enters the believer, by faith, into the status of adoption: "As many as received him, to them gave he power to become the sons of God, even to them that believe on his name: which were born, not of blood, nor of the will of the flesh, nor of the will of man, but of God" (John 1:12–13).[12] From the moment of regeneration and faith, the believer is spiritually united with Christ as part of the Son of God's body and is thus judged by the Father to be one of His adopted children (Eph. 1:23).[13] Willard summarizes, "*Though we were appointed to it [adoption] from Eternity, yet it is conferred upon us in Believing.*"[14]

The believer may also subjectively realize adoption. "There must in order of nature be the *certitude*

---

11. *Works of Boston,* 1:619, 621.
12. *Works of Manton,* 12:123.
13. Brakel, *Christian's Reasonable Service,* 2:420.
14. Willard, *A Compleat Body of Divinity,* 487.

objecti, before *certitude subjecti,* for I can never be sure of a thing before it is," writes Ford. Years may transpire, he goes on to say, before the believer who is adopted by God may *know* he is adopted. In fact, since the subjective consciousness of adoption is not essential to eternal life, Ford concludes it is *possible* — not normative — that a believer "may go to heaven without that particular actual assurance, or a particular confidence to addresse himself to God as his Father."[15]

The Puritans believed that all God did outside of the Christian for his salvation has its counterpart within him. The Christ who merited salvation for His elect also applies it to them. This He does by what John Forbes called His "experienced word": God "speakes the word of trueth to the heart," causes the heart "to believe that which it hath heard and received," and adds "his spirit: and by the testimonie thereof...makes Adoption and eternall life, most certain and sure to the soule."[16]

The witnessing testimony of the Spirit

Most Puritans were fond of calling this certainty the witnessing testimony of the Holy Spirit, which they usually identified with the consciousness of the sealing

15. Ford, *The Spirit of Bondage and Adoption,* 201–202.

16. Forbes, *How a Christian man may discerne the testimonie of Gods spirit, from the testimonie of his owne spirit, in witnessing his Adoption,* 37.

of the Spirit and assurance of faith. The Westminster Confession of Faith refers to "the testimony of the Spirit of adoption witnessing with our spirit that we are the children of God" (XVIII:ii). In his 200-page book on the witnessing of the Spirit written five years after the completion of the Westminster Assembly, Samuel Petto defines the Spirit's witnessing ministry as "a worke whereby the Spirit doth that towards the clearing up unto a soule of its Adoption, that a witnes doth amongst men for the decision and determination of a matter dubious and uncertaine."[17]

The Puritans vary in their interpretations of how the Spirit's witnessing testimony is experienced by the child of God.[18] Some, such as Jeremiah Burroughs, Anthony Burgess, and George Gillespie, emphasize that the witnessing testimony of the Holy Spirit coincides with assurance gleaned from inward evidences of grace, which the Puritans also call the marks or fruits of grace.[19] They believe that the Spirit's witness refers exclusively to His activity of uniting the adopted child's conscience with the Spirit's witness that the Christian is a child of God. According to that view, the witness of the Holy Spirit conjoins

---

17. Petto, *The Voice of the Spirit,* 7.

18. This is expounded in more detail in my *Quest for Full Assurance: The Legacy of Calvin and His Successors* (Edinburgh: Banner of Truth Trust, 1999), 142–47.

19. Burroughs, *The Saints' Happiness,* 196; Burgess, *Spiritual Refining,* 44; Gillespie, *A Treatise of Miscellany Questions* (Edinburgh: Gedeon Lithgovv, for George Svvintuun, 1649), 105–109.

with the witness of the believer's spirit. Romans 8:15 (receiving the Spirit of adoption) and 8:16 (the Spirit's bearing witness together with the believer's conscience) are thus synonymous.[20] Thus, when the Spirit's witness and the witness of the believer's conscience unitedly confirm that the believer possesses the marks and fruits of grace to some degree, the believer, assured that he is a child, may then cry out, "Abba, Father" (Gal. 4:6).[21]

Thomas Manton describes the Spirit's witness with our spirit in six thoughts:

(1) The Spirit lays down marks [of grace] in scripture.

(2) He worketh such graces as are peculiar to God's children, and are evidences of our interest in the favour of God.

(3) He helpeth us to feel and discover those acts in ourselves.

(4) The Spirit helps us to compare them with the rule [of Scripture], and accordingly to judge of their sincerity.

(5) The Spirit helps us to conclude rightly of our estate.

(6) He enlivens and heightens our apprehensions in all these particulars, and so fills us with com-

---

20. Cf. Perkins's exegesis of Romans 8:16 in *Works of Perkins,* 2:18–19; Burgess's exegesis of Romans 8:15–16, Ephesians 1:13, and 1 John 5:8 in *Spiritual Refining,* 49–50.

21. Cf. *Works of Perkins,* 2:277–80; *Works of Owen,* 4:265–70.

fort, and raiseth our joy upon the feeling of the sense of the favour of God; for all this is the fruit of his operation.[22]

Other Puritans, such as Samuel Petto, Samuel Rutherford, William Twisse, Henry Scudder, Herman Witsius, Thomas Cole, and Cotton Mather, concur with much of what has been said thus far, but they feel that all this is included in the previous expression in WCF XVIII:ii, which refers to assurance obtained through the inward evidences of grace. They believe that the witnessing testimony of the Spirit involves something more; the witness of the Spirit described in Romans 8:15 contains something distinct from that of verse 16.[23] They distinguish the Spirit's witness *with* the believer's spirit from His witnessing *to* the believer's spirit by direct applications of the Word. As Heinrich Meyer pointed out, the former works the self-conscious conviction, "*I* am a child of God," and thus finds freedom to approach God as Father. The latter involves the Spirit's pronouncement on behalf

---

22. *Works of Manton,* 1:51–53.

23. Petto, *The Voice of the Spirit,* 67–97; Rutherford, *The Covenant of Life Opened, or A Treatise of the Covenant of Grace* (Edinburgh: Andro Anderson, for Robert Broun, 1655), 65ff.; Twisse, *The Doctrine of the Synod of Dort and Arles, reduced to the practice* (Amsterdam: G.Thorp, 1631), 147ff.; Scudder, *The Christian's Daily Walk, in holy Security and Peace* (reprint, Harrisburg, Va.: Sprinkle, 1984), 338–42; Witsius, *Economy of the Covenants,* 1:465ff.; Cole, *Christ the Foundation of our Adoption,* 357–62; Mather, *The Sealed Servants of our God, Appearing with Two Witnesses,* 16–22.

of the Father, "*You* are a child of God," and thus approaches the Father with the familiarity of a child, crying out, "Abba, Father," on the basis of hearing one's own sonship pronounced from God's Word.[24] Herman Witsius says that this comes with such power, "immediately assuring God's beloved people of their adoption, no less than if they were carried up to the third heavens, and had heard it audibly from God's own mouth."[25] Cotton Mather distinguishes these two grounds of assurance this way:

> There is a *Testimony* of the Holy SPIRIT unto our *Adoption,* which comes as a *Mighty Light,* more *Directly* breaking in upon our Minds, to assure us, that we are indeed the *Adopted* of GOD. There is a *Discursive Assurance* of our Blessedness; which is drawn from the *Marks* and *Signs* of a Soul become an *Habitation of God thro' the Spirit.* And then ther is a more *Intuitive Assurance* of it; In which the Holy SPIRIT, more Immediately, and most Irresistibly, and with a *Mighty Light,* bears in upon the Mind of the Beleever a power-ful perswasion of it, That he is a *Child* of GOD, and his GOD and *Father* will one day bring him to *Inherit all things.* The Soul of the Beleever is now wonderfully moved and melted and overpowered with such Thoughts as these; *GOD is my Father,*

---

24. Meyer, *Critical and Exegetical Hand-book to The Epistle of the Romans* (New York: Funk & Wagnalls, 1889), 316.

25. Witsius, *Economy of the Covenants,* 1:466–67.

*CHRIST is my Saviour, and I have an Inheritance
in the Heavens reserved for me.*[26]

However the Puritans may have varied here, they
all agreed that the Spirit is essential in every aspect
of adoption and assurance, and that the Spirit's testimony is always tied to, and may never contradict, the
Word of God.[27] They knew that without Word and
Spirit at work, all spiritual experience is counterfeit
and can easily degenerate into a host of errors, such
as unbiblical mysticism, excessive emotionalism,
introspective bondage, or barren antinomianism.

Growing in the consciousness of adoption

The mature child of God, therefore, grows in the consciousness of his adoption and assurance through
Word and Spirit. His own thoughts and conscience
become increasingly shaped by the new life within
him, promoting an inward conviction that he is a
Christian.

That growth has some ups and downs, however.
Simon Ford says, "Of those that have this assurance and enlargement thereupon, very few or none
keep it *at all times alike,* and can alike improve it
on every occasion. Great sinnes, and great troubles
&c. may many times cloud, and sometimes as to the

---

26. Mather, *The Sealed Servants of our God, Appearing with
Two Witnesses,* 16.

27. *Works of Manton,* 12:127; Witsius, *Economy of the
Covenants,* 1:463; Petto, *The Voice of the Spirit,* 23–41.

act, blot out the evidence of their Adoption. Thus *David* wanted this Spirit, *Psal.* 51.11.12. A child having offended, may scarce dare call Father, whiles that guilt remains uncovered."[28]

Manton puts it succinctly: "The workman that made a thing can best warrant it to the buyer. First he [the Spirit] sanctifieth, and then he certifieth; sometimes we overlook our evidences through the darkness and confusion that is in our hearts." He goes on to say that the Spirit "helpeth us not only to see grace, but to judge of the sincerity of grace." The Spirit helps us conclude with boldness, comfort, and joy from the evidences of our lives that we are adopted sons or daughters of God. This comfort enables us to pray and embrace God's promises with freedom.[29] Those divine promises always remain the primary ground of the assurance of our adoption. The Spirit comforts us with God's promises of our adoption — Ford explains how He does this by using such promises as Psalm 126:5–6 and Isaiah 61:1–3 — and grants us grace to apply them to ourselves.[30]

Such believers are advised by the Puritans to hold fast their profession, to grow in the grace and knowledge of Jesus Christ, to witness of the Father's goodness to others, and to lead lives of service to God and man. In short, as adopted children they

---

28. Ford, *The Spirit of Bondage and Adoption*, 201.

29. *Works of Manton*, 12:128–29.

30. Ford, *The Spirit of Bondage and Adoption*, 204–205.

should daily engage in the responsibilities and duties expounded below in chapter 11.

The question we need to ask is, have we been born again and become part of that new creation in Christ Jesus whereby old things have passed away and all things have become new? Apart from that, adoption will never mean anything to us.

CHAPTER EIGHT

◆

The Marks of Adoption

The Puritans gave clear marks for us to determine to which family we belong, God's or Satan's. They believed that when self-examination is undertaken biblically, the Holy Spirit often uses it as a positive transforming power in the lives of God's children.

William Perkins provides six marks that may help certify one's adoption:

- An earnest and heartie desire in all things to further the glorie of God.

- A care and readiness to resigne our selues in subjection to God, to bee ruled by his word and spirit, in thought, word, and deede.

- A sincere endeauor to do his will in all things with cheerfulnesse, making conscience of euerything we know to be euill.

- Vpright walking in a mans lawfull calling, and yet still by faith to relie vpon Gods prouidence, being well pleased with Gods sending whatsoeuer it is.

- Euery day to humble a mans selfe before God for his offences, seeking his fauour in Christ vnfainedly, and so daily renuing his faith & repentance.

- A continual combate between the flesh and the spirt, corruption haling and drawing one way, and grace resisting the same & drawing another way.[1]

Roger Drake offers these marks: a spirit of faith and dependency (2 Cor. 4:13); a spirit of prayer (Acts 9:11); a spirit of evidence (Rom. 8:16); a spirit of liberty (2 Cor. 3:17); a spirit of waiting (Rom. 8:23); and a spirit of love (1 John 5:2).[2] Thomas Cole speaks of "a loving peaceable disposition, a spiritual and holy Conversation, a reverential fear of God in all our ways, and a restless breathing and panting after God when he hides his face from us in any displeasure."[3]

Thomas Boston said that we may know what family we belong to by considering the image we bear, the spirit we convey, and the affections we have for the family of God.[4] Thomas Watson highlights three marks of grace: uniform obedience by faith to God's glory, love to be in our Father's presence, and evidences of being led by God's Spirit.[5] Wilhelmus à Brakel also provides three marks on sonship: saving faith, bearing the Father's image, and having "inner motions which only belong to a child of God." Under inner motions, Brakel includes to love the Father, to

---

1. *Works of Perkins,* 3:154.
2. *Puritan Sermons,* 5:344.
3. Cole, *Christ the Foundation of our Adoption,* 346–49.
4. *Works of Boston,* 1:629–35.
5. Watson, *A Body of Practical Divinity,* 158–59.

desire to be in His presence, to be humbled before Him, to be willing to do His will, and to love all His children.[6] Cotton Mather says that we belong to God's family when we can positively answer that our only trust for salvation lies in Jesus Christ and His atoning blood, that we are effectually called by the Spirit, and that we exercise vital piety, which consists of fearing God, giving glory to Him, and loving our neighbor.[7] Stephen Marshall said we must answer questions like these: "Is the Holy Ghost come to dwel in you to unite you to Christ? Doth the Holy Ghost work a Childs heart in you? Can you honor God, and reverence him, and turn to him? And can you walk before God as obedient Children, at least in the constant bent and tenure of your Souls?"[8]

Herman Witsius divides the marks of self-examination into two kinds: "first, a certain good habit or disposition of soul, with a consistent tenour of a pious life." This includes the impression and expression of the divine image, with a holy conformity to our Father and Elder Brother; a new life that is worthy of God and the effect of the Spirit of adoption; a true and sincere love of God; a filial fear and obedience, and unfeigned brotherly love. Second, there are marks of adoption that are "peculiar acts

---

6. Brakel, *Christian's Reasonable Service*, 2:427–33.

7. Mather, *The Sealed Servants of our God, Appearing with Two Witnesses*, 9ff.

8. *Works of Marshall*, 54–55.

of God towards his beloved people, which he vouch-
safes only to those whom he loves as a Father." These
acts include such times of blessed communion with
God that are rare for His children. Here is Witsius's
description of these blessed times:

> While they are sometimes ravished on high by
> his Spirit, he surrounds them with the beams of
> his supercelestial light, gives them a view of his
> face shining with the brightest love, kisses them
> with the kisses of his mouth, admits them to the
> most endearing, mutual intercourse of mystical
> love with himself, and, while he plentifully sheds
> abroad his love in their hearts, he gives them to
> drink of rivers of honey and butter, and that often
> in the greatest drought of the parched soul, when
> expecting no such things. There are many more
> mysteries in this secret intercourse with our heav-
> enly Father, which believers sometimes see, taste,
> and feel, and which no pen of the learned can rep-
> resent, as they deserve.

Witsius hastens to add that if a child of God
misses such times, he ought not despair; but if he
experiences such times, he will be even more assured
that he belongs to God's family. When we experience "the peculiar favour of the most gracious God,
exciting, inflaming, comforting, and carrying heav-
enwards our otherwise dull and drowsy hearts," we
entirely acquiesce to the testimony of our own spirit
being "superadded [to] that of the Spirit of God."[9]

---

9. Witsius, *Economy of the Covenants,* 1:465–66.

———— ♦ ————

CHAPTER NINE

Transformed Relationships in Adoption

The consciousness of personal adoption into God's family influences the entire life of the believer. The Puritans would agree with Packer: "Sonship must be the controlling thought — the normative category, if you like — at every point."[1] Every relationship in the believer's life is transformed by it.

Christ Himself is the best proof of this truth. Jesus' consciousness of His unique filial relationship with the Father controlled all of Christ's living and thinking: "I seek not mine own will, but the will of the Father which hath sent me" (John 5:30); "If I do not the works of my Father, believe me not," Jesus says in John 10:37, and "As my Father hath sent me, even so send I you" (John 20:21). Jesus likewise urges His disciples to let their thoughts and lives be controlled by the conviction that God is now their Father and they are His children, and that He knows all their

---

1. Packer, *Knowing God,* 190.

needs (Matt. 6:32). The child of God is to pray and to live his whole life in relation to his Father, remembering that the Father has promised each child His kingdom.

John Cotton makes plain in expounding 1 John 3 that the significance of adoption affects the following relationships:

1. *Our relationship to God* (1 John 3:1a). In addition to what has already been stated, God's adopted children learn that the only place in the universe where true security can be found is in the household of the heavenly Father, who is the God and Father of our Lord Jesus Christ. Nothing in life is secure except God. He alone does not change (Mal. 3:6). Jesus taught His disciples this truth in many ways. For example, He urged them to think about God's fatherly love by comparing it to the love of a human father: "If ye then, being evil, know how to give good gifts unto your children, how much more shall your Father which is in heaven give good things to them that ask him?" (Matt. 7:11).

   The comparison is between the imperfect fatherhood of earthly fathers, who are evil (i.e., they have fallen natures and show flaws, failures, and sins) and the fatherhood of God, which is steadfast and flawless. Our shortcomings incline us to confess with Cotton that "surely I am not a child of God, because I find much pride in my heart, and much rebellion and corruption in my spirit. Surely if I were born of Christ, I should be like him. But what says St. John here? We are the sons of God even now, though there is much unbelief in our hearts, and much weakness and many corruptions within us."[2] Despite all this, Jesus will show us that our heavenly Father's love is expansive and glorious beyond imagination. Every sphere of our lives must be lived in relation to God as our Father.

2. *Our relationship to the world.* The believer's adoption by God the Father also affects his relationship to the world. First John 3:1b tells us that this relationship is a troubled one: "Therefore the world knoweth us not, because it knew him not." On the one hand, the believer shares with Jesus the unspeakable love of the Father, but on the other hand, he shares with Jesus the hostility, estrangement, and even hatred of the world.

This reaction of the world is one evidence of the believer's adoption into God's family, for the world did not know Jesus either; "he came unto his own and his own received him not" (John 1:11). He was in the world He created, but the world knew Him not. The world did not recognize Him as the Son of God; ultimately, it crucified Him. "If God saw it meet that his Son should be thus afflicted in the world and drink of such a bitter portion of God's wrath," writes Cotton, "let us not think we shall go to heaven and partake of those heavenly mansions which Christ has prepared for us, without also drinking of the same cup that he drank of. Let us account ourselves happy that God will so esteem us as to make us his sons."[3]

When a sinner is born again and brought into

---

2. John Cotton, *An Exposition of First John* (reprint Evansville, Ind.: Sovereign Grace Publishers, 1962), 319.

3. Ibid., 318.

God's family, he discovers that worldly people no longer understand him. Believers and unbelievers live in different worlds, in different kingdoms, in different families. This separation brings consequences; nevertheless, God will uphold His adopted children. Cotton says, "Though the children of God be afflicted and weather-beaten, yet God has promised blessings to them which make them blessed in the world (1 John 3:13–14)."[4] Adoption into God's family means that we must be willing for Christ's sake to endure being misunderstood, unwanted, despised, even hated, by the world, all the while striving to give no unnecessary offense to the world.

3. *Our relationship to the future.* We cherish a great hope. John goes on to say, "Beloved, now are we the sons of God, and it doth not yet appear what we shall be: but we know that, when he shall appear, we shall be like him; for we shall see him as he is" (1 John 3:2). The prospects for God's adopted family are great, for His children will receive a glorious inheritance. They cannot even imagine the extent of that inheritance, which God keeps hidden, says Cotton, so that they may (1) be like their suffering Head, (2) have their faith kept in exercise and be watchful, and (3) be tolerated to some degree in this world, for "if God should allow them to be perfectly holy in this world, the men of the world would not allow them to live among them long (Deut. 7:22)."[5]

    God's child is like a poor peasant who has been

---

4. Ibid., 318.

5. Ibid., 320–21.

taken out of the mire and raised to the position of prince of the realm. The adopted prince lives in the palace, has free access to the king, and enjoys the king's favor, love, and protection. The prince tells the king that he cannot comprehend the greatness of the king's love; it is unspeakably great to him. The king responds: "You have not begun to see the extent of it. Your inheritance is still coming to you."

If our present privileges as God's adopted children are so great that the world cannot grasp them, our future prospects are so glorious that even we cannot fully grasp them. As 1 Corinthians 2:9 says, "Eye hath not seen, nor ear heard, neither have entered into the heart of man, the things which God hath prepared for them that love him." Because God is our Father and we are His adopted children, we have a full inheritance awaiting us. The best is yet to be. Today we experience great blessings, despite our infirmities and sins; but one day we will be in glory, free from sin and living in perfect communion with God. Our heavenly Father keeps the best surprises for His children until the end, when He will turn all their sorrow into joy.

Moreover, God is shaping us to share in the glories of our Lord Jesus Christ. As 1 John 3:2 says, "When he shall appear, we shall be like him; for we shall see him as he is." God is changing us now, but then we will be so changed that we will fully bear His image without spot or wrinkle. Paul tells us in Romans 8 that the whole creation waits for the day when the inheritance of the children of God will be given to them. What a future!

4. *Our relationship to ourselves.* The children of the heavenly Father embrace His will and purpose for them. Every adopted child of God also knows that

holiness is an important part of God's purpose for his happiness in God's family. First John 3:3 says, "Every man that hath this hope in him purifieth himself, even as he is pure." Cotton draws this doctrine from this text: "Every child of God has hope in Christ, to be made like him at his appearing." That hope is "a patient, certain, and grounded expectation of all those promises in Christ which by faith we believe to belong to us." God gives this hope through the means of grace so that we "might not be tossed and hurried up and down the world."[6]

So we are to purify ourselves daily, using Christ as our pattern. Colossians 3 tells us that holiness means putting off everything that is dishonoring to our Father, who has loved us, and the Savior, who has died to save us. It means putting on "mercies, kindness, humbleness of mind, meekness, and longsuffering" (3:12). Purifying ourselves involves "the whole man," says Cotton, including what we do with our minds, affections, wills, thoughts, tongues, eyes, hands, disappointments, injuries, and enemies.[7] Purifying ourselves involves loving all that the Father loves and hating all that the Father hates. From the moment of conversion to the time we take our final breath, we have one pursuit: to purify ourselves before our Father in order to be more like Christ.

The Greek word for *purify* refers to undivided allegiance, or having one's eyes focused on a single goal. It implies wholeness and singleness of purpose. It means having undivided motives in our living and our service, being wholly dedicated

6. Ibid., 327–29.
7. Ibid., 331.

to living a life that glorifies Jesus Christ. One way Christians become known as sons of God is by having a new goal for themselves, a new relationship toward themselves. By God's grace, they purify themselves, even as Christ is pure.

5. *Our relationship to the church as the family of God.* As God's adopted sons and daughters, we have been placed in a great family. If we rightly understand this, our attitude toward our brothers and sisters in the family of God will be profoundly affected (1 John 3:14–18). We have not been adopted to live apart from that family, but to live within its network of relationships. God's purpose in adopting children is to create a family in which Christ will be glorified as the firstborn among many brethren. He wants the love that exists between the Father and the Son and the Holy Spirit to be extended through the love between brothers and sisters in Christ. As Cotton says, "the sons of God ought to be the men of our love and delight (3 John 1, 2, 5; 1 Pet. 2:11; Phil. 4:1)."[8]

The communion of saints is essential to the proclamation and vindication of the gospel. That is why it is so grievous when people in the church do not show love to one another. If we profess a Savior who laid down His life for us and we are part of His family, we ought to be willing to lay down our lives for other members of the family.[9] We should uphold them, serve them, and sacrifice for them. We should not grieve each other, wound each other, or gossip about each

---

8. Ibid., 316.
9. Ibid., 379.

other. We must love in "deed and in truth; not [merely] in tongue, but in truth of inward affection and deed and performance."[10] The way we behave toward other Christians proves whether or not we are adopted children of God (3:14–15). We are to love fellow adoptees of God, Cotton says, because of (1) "God's singular love to them," (2) "their love to God," and (3) "the truth that is in every Christian believer (2 John 1, 2)."[11]

If we show little love to other children of God, we prove that we have tasted little of God's love in our lives, for those who have experienced much love from Him cannot help but love others. As Cotton concludes, "The lack of love to any of our brethren is a sign of abiding in the state of damnation, or in an unregenerate and carnal state."[12]

---

10. Ibid., 383.
11. Ibid., 317.
12. Ibid., 372.

———— ♦ ————

CHAPTER TEN

The Privileges and Benefits of Adoption

The Puritans spend more time expounding what are variously called the privileges, liberties, benefits, blessings, or rights of adoption than any other aspect of adoption. This is also evident in the Westminster Confession of Faith (XII) and Larger Catechism (Q. 74), where more than half of the material on adoption is devoted to a listing of these "liberties and privileges," each of which the Spirit uses to exercise His transforming power and comfort in the lives of God's children.

The overarching privilege can best be summarized as *heirship*. God's adopted children are all royal heirs apparent and coheirs with Christ (Rom. 8:16–17). "Men may have many children yet but one is an heir," writes Burroughs. "But all the children of God are heirs."[1] Hebrews 12:23 calls them "firstborn" heirs.

The Puritans make much of joint-heirship with

---

1. Burroughs, *The Saints' Happiness,* 192.

Christ. Listen to Burroughs again, speaking to believers: "I say, whatsoever thou art in the world, Jesus Christ is not an heir to more than thou hast an interest in. Thou art as certain of thy salvation and glory as it is certain that Jesus Christ shall be happy for ever; because thou art a co-heir with Jesus Christ. You know, when men are co-heirs, the title of one is as certain as the other. If you be but a co-purchaser with another, then you have as true a right in such a land or house as they have...ay, but it is more to be a co-heir than a co-purchaser: the right of inheritance is better and a more noble right than the right of purchase." Burroughs revels in this truth: "Oh, who can utter the soul-satisfying, soul-ravishing consolation there is in this, that the same God that is the God of Jesus Christ is my God, and the same Father that is the Father of Jesus Christ is my Father!"[2]

As coheirs with Christ, believers share in Christ's kingship, and therefore they partake of the kingdom of heaven as their inheritance. Believers are made kings of the Father in His spiritual kingdom in three respects, writes Thomas Granger. "1. Because they are Lords and Conquerors of their enemies, Sinne, Satan, the World, Death, Hell. 2. They are partakers of the kingdome of Christ and of saluation; for wee haue receiued of Christ grace for grace, and glorie for glorie. 3. They haue interest, dominion, and

---

soueraigntie of all things by Christ."[3] Witsius stresses that this "all things" includes the right of "possession of the whole world," which was given to but lost by Adam (Gen. 1:28; 3:24), promised to Abraham (Rom. 4:13), and repurchased by Christ "for himself and his brethren" (cf. Ps. 8:6), so that now all things, both present and to come, are His people's.[4]

Samuel Willard says that "God is theirs, Christ is theirs, the Throne and Crown that are prepared, and the exceeding eternal weight of Glory are theirs."[5] Stephen Marshall adds: "Whatsoever is in this world is for their sakes, the Angels, the World, the Devils in Hel, inspite of their Hearts they are al under the Saints."[6] Ultimately, believers are lords and possessors of all things, because they belong to Christ who belongs to God (1 Cor. 3:21–23).[7] "All that a Believer enjoys in this life he may truly call his own, as he is a child of God," writes Willard. Believers "have a spiritual right [to all they possess], and all their enjoyments are theirs by the new Covenant."[8]

Believers receive this kingly inheritance through the death of their Testator, Jesus Christ. By Spirit-worked faith, they appropriate this inheritance to

---

3. Granger, *A Looking Glasse for Christians,* [26].

4. Witsius, *Economy of the Covenants,* 1:452–53.

5. Willard, *The Child's Portion,* 29.

6. *Works of Marshall,* 52.

7. *Workes of Perkins,* 1:82, 369.

8. Willard, *The Child's Portion,* 27.

themselves, though they are altogether unworthy of it. Granger draws these helpful comparisons: In natural life, the adopter is often moved to bequeath his inheritance because of some worth in the adopted, but the Father finds in us no motive for His love. In natural life, the adopter gives money or lands, but the Father gives His own Son. In natural life, the adopter cannot give "the spirit of a naturall sonne to the adopted; but God hath giuen vnto us the spirit of sonnes, by whom we call him (*Abba*) Father." In natural life, the adopted may love the adopter only outwardly, but "the children of God are vnited vnto him in the inward affection of heart."[9]

Nothing in this world can match the inheritance of believers. It knows no *corruption* (1 Peter 1:4) — not "by outward principles, as fire, violence, &c.; nor by inward principles, as sin and other taints which defile" (cf. Isa. 29:14; 1 Peter 1:18). It has no *succession*. The heavenly Father and His children always live out of the same inheritance, so the believers' inheritance is as unchangeable as Christ's priesthood is (Heb. 7:24). It faces no *division*. Every heir enjoys the whole inheritance, since God is both "infinite and indivisible." "God gives His all, not half, but his whole kingdom" (cf. Gen. 25:5; Rev. 21:7).[10]

Specific blessings that accrue for us as believers

9. Granger, *A Looking Glasse for Christians,* [22–23].

10. Drake, *Puritan Sermons,* 5:334; cf. *Works of Owen,* 2:218–21, and Burroughs, *The Saints' Happiness,* 196.

from His divine inheritance and spiritual adoption include the most wonderful privileges one could ever imagine, both in this world and in the world to come. Here is a summary of them, drawn from the Puritans:

• Our Father cuts us off from the family to which we naturally belong in Adam as children of wrath and of the devil, and He ingrafts us into His own family to make us members of the covenant family of God. "Adoption translates us out of a Miserable estate, into a Happy estate," writes Thomas Cole. "God is in covenant with us, and we in him."[11] By nature, Stephen Marshall says, we are "Children of wrath, Children of Belial, Children of old Adam, Children of Sin and Death, we are cut off from that Family, no longer to reckoned of it, [or of its] Bondage, Baseness, Obligations, Curses" and are "taken into Gods Family as his Sons and Daughters, that is,...he hath ingaged himself perpetually forever" to us, so that this family relationship will last forever (John 8:35).[12]

As believers, therefore, we are one household, called the household of faith (Gal. 6:10).[13] Believers become our brothers and sisters in the most wonderful family that exists in this world.[14] We are one in

---

11. Cole, *Christ the Foundation of our Adoption,* 351.

12. *Works of Marshall,* 50–51.

13. Willard, *The Child's Portion,* 15.

14. Granger, *A Looking Glasse for Christians,* [24].

Christ Jesus. As adopted children, we are invested with all the rights and privileges in God's family that earthly adopted children possess in their own family.[15]

• Our Father gives us freedom to call on Him by His Father-name and gives us a new name, which serves as our guarantee of admission to the house of God as sons and daughters of God (Rev. 2:17; 3:12). We are a peculiar people — His people, called by His name (2 Chron. 7:14). That means, says Thomas Boston, that our "old name is for ever laid aside. [We] are no more called children of the devil, but the sons and daughters of God" (Heb. 12:5). John Cotton goes a step further, saying expressly that this name is *Adoption:* "[We] have this white Stone, that is Absolution for sin, and in that a new name written, that is, Adoption: and if we be of a meek, humble, innocent, frame of mind, we have this comfort."[16] By the Spirit of adoption, we have access to God as a reconciled Father through Christ. We have liberty to call God Father, which "is more worth than a thousand worlds" (cf. Jer. 3:4).[17]

---

15. *Works of Owen,* 2:216–17.

16. Cited in Jesper Rosenmeir, "'Clearing the Medium': A Reevaluation of the Puritan Plain Style in Light of John Cotton's *A Practicall Commentary Upon the First Epistle Generall of John,*" *William and Mary Quarterly,* 37, no. 4 (1980), 582.

17. *Works of Boston,* 1:623.

The adopted also have Christ's name put on them (Eph. 3:15). Thomas Ridgley says that "this signifies not only that propriety which he has in them as Mediator, but their relation to him as the ransomed of the Lord,— his sheep, whom he leads, and feeds like a shepherd. They are also styled his children, when he says, 'Behold I and the children which God hath given me'" (Heb. 2:13).[18]

• Our Father gifts us with the Spirit of adoption. Believers are, by grace, partakers of the Holy Spirit. This Spirit, Burroughs tells us, enlightens our mind, sanctifies our heart, makes God's wisdom and will known to us, guides us to eternal life, yes, works the entire work of salvation in us and seals it to us unto the day of redemption (Eph. 4:30).[19]

The Westminster Confession of Faith overtly links the Spirit's ministry of adoption with assurance. An infallible assurance of faith is found, in part, on "the testimony of the Spirit of adoption witnessing with our spirits that we are the children of God" (XVIII: ii; Rom. 8:15 –16). Willard writes that the Spirit "ratifies our Sonship to be immutable, and confirms our title to all the Promises irreversible. As such a Spirit, he gives his testimony in us, to ratify all our evidences, and fully assure us of our Sonship and Heirship."[20]

---

18. Ridgley, *Commentary on the Larger Catechism*, 2:135.
19. Burroughs, *The Saints' Happiness*, 196.
20. Willard, *A Compleat Body of Divinity*, 489.

• Our Father grants us likeness to Himself and His Son. The Father imparts to His children a filial heart and disposition that resemble His own. Roger Drake writes that "all God's adopted children bear their Father's image, as Gideon's brethren did his (Judg. 8:18). They are like God, in holiness [and] in dignity" (Matt. 5:44–45; Rom. 8:29; Heb. 2:7; 1 John 3:2–3).[21]

Thomas Cole writes similarly from a Christological perspective: "Christ is formed in them all, *Gal. 4.19.* As Christ is, so are they, each one resembles the children of a King, *Judg. 8.18.* They will be exactly like Christ as the Resurrection, *Psal. 17.15. They were from Eternity predestinated unto this,* Rom. 8.29."[22] Anthony Burgess reminds us that this includes the privilege of being "made conformable unto Christ in his sufferings" (cf. Phil. 1:29).[23]

• Our Father especially strengthens our faith through His gifts of promises and prayer. "If we are adopted," writes Thomas Watson, "then we have an interest in all the promises: the promises are children's bread." They are like a garden, Watson goes on to say, in which some herb is found to cure every ailment.[24] Or,

---

21. Drake, *Puritan Sermons,* 5:333.

22. Cole, *Christ the Foundation of our Adoption,* 350; cf. Burroughs, *The Saints' Happiness,* 195–96.

23. Burgess, *Spiritual Refining,* 242.

24. Watson, *A Body of Practical Divinity,* 160.

as William Spurstowe put it, God's promises are like a bag full of coins that God unties and pours out at the feet of His adopted children, saying, "Take what you will."[25]

Concerning prayer, we are given limitless access to our heavenly Father. Children have the right of access to their father, no matter how busy or important he is — even if he is president of the nation. So, in the New Testament, adopted sons are encouraged to come boldly to the throne of grace through the God-man Savior at any time to find grace and mercy to help in time of need (Heb. 4:14–16), notwithstanding the exaltedness of their God.

The Spirit teaches us that the Father in heaven is more pleased to see His adopted children come through the door of prayer into His throne room than we are pleased to see our children come through the door into our living room. Willard writes that the Spirit "enlivens" the faith of believers, enabling them "to go to God as a Father, and claim this relation, and upon the claim, believingly to plead with him for the acceptance of their persons, the audience of their Prayers, the granting of their requests, and supplying of all their wants" (Rom. 8:15).[26] Boston says, "As

---

25. William Spurstowe, *The Wells of Salvation Opened: or A Treatise discovering the nature, preciousness, and usefulness, of the Gospel Promises, and Rules for the Right Application of them* (London: T. R. & E. M. for Ralph Smith, 1655), 34ff.

26. Willard, *The Child's Portion*, 21.

children, [they] pour their complaints into his bosom, and tell him all their wants."[27] Brakel says, "The Lord looks upon such children in love, and is pleased with their childlike complaints and their taking refuge to Him. He will most certainly answer them and deliver them at His time and in His manner" (Luke 11:13).[28]

• Our Father corrects and chastens us for our sanctification. "He chasteneth and scourgeth every son whom he receiveth" (Heb. 12:6). All chastisements involves discipline that comes from our Father's hand and works together for our best welfare (2 Sam. 7:14; Ps. 89:32–33; Rom. 8:28, 36–37; 2 Cor. 12:7). Our sufferings are "for our education and instruction in his family," writes Owen;[29] or, as Willard puts it, "All our afflictions are helps toward heaven." They contribute to the "increase of their eternal glory: every reproach and injury doth but add weight to their Crown."[30] We foolishly think that God chastens us to destroy us, but 1 Corinthians 11:32 teaches us that "we are chastened of the Lord, that we should not be condemned with the world."[31]

Thomas Boston says of the Father's chasten-

---

27. *Works of Boston,* 1:624.

28. Brakel, *Christian's Reasonable Service,* 2:423.

29. *Works of Owen,* 24:257.

30. Willard, *The Child's Portion,* 28.

31. *Workes of Perkins,* 1:82; Willard, *The Child's Portion,* 18–19; Granger, *A Looking Glasse for Christians,* [31–32].

ing of His people: "When he corrects them, he does it with a fatherly reluctance, Lam. iii. 33. When he gives them a frown or a rough word, his bowels yearn towards them, and their relentings go near his heart, Jer. xxx. 20."[32] God's chastenings, then, are badges of our sonship and of the Father's love (Heb. 12:3–11). They are meant only for believers in this life. Owen says that "there is no chastisement in heaven, nor in hell. Not in heaven, because there is no sin; not in hell, because there is no amendment."[33]

• Our Father comforts us with His love and pity, and He moves us to rejoice in intimate communion with Him and His Son (Rom. 5:5). He does this in several ways, as Willard notes: "He applies the precious promises to their souls, he gives them cordials of comfort, communicates unto them the sips and foretasts of glory, [and] fills them with inward joyes and refreshings."[34] The Father commends and encourages us even for the smallest act of obedience.[35] He comforts us in accord with the afflictions He has measured out for us.[36]

Our Father distinguishes weakness from wickedness in us, and He shows compassion (Ps. 103:13).

---

32. *Works of Boston,* 1:625.
33. *Works of Owen,* 24:260.
34. Willard, *The Child's Portion,* 22.
35. Ibid., 19.
36. *Workes of Perkins,* 1:369.

Boston writes that "no bowels are so tender and lasting as God's towards his children; no mother so tender of the fruit of her womb as God is of his children, Isa. xlix. 15."[37]

But what if we cannot always feel that love? Should we not then question the Father's love to us and our adoption by Him? Thomas Shepard responds, "Is thy son not thy child, because while it is young it knows not the father that begot it, or because thou art sometimes departed from it, and has it not always in thine own arms?"[38]

How precious then is the love of the heavenly Father toward His children! Jeremiah Burroughs writes, "God, who is the infinite glorious first-being, embraces them with an entire fatherly love. All the love that ever was in any parents towards children, is but as one drop of the infinite ocean of fatherly love that there is in God unto his people."[39]

• Our Father assists us in performing spiritual duties acceptably by the Spirit of adoption, particularly the duty of prayer to God (Rom. 8:26–27). Willard says that though God's children carry about "a masse of corruption, a body of Death, which presseth them down," the Spirit "stands by them, and is ready to put to his helping hand, supplying them with the influ-

---

37. *Works of Boston*, 1:625.

38. Shepard, *The Sound Believer*, 253.

39. Burroughs, *The Saints' Happiness*, 194.

ences of spiritual Grace, whence, when they are weak in themselves, they are strong in him."[40] As God's children, believers receive liberty and boldness in prayer to God, Jesus having opened the way. They come without sacrifices and human priests, trusting only in the offering of Jesus (Heb. 10:14; 7:19). They do not have to stand at a distance from their Father and wait to be asked to approach; they can now, for Christ's sake, leap into and rest in their Father's bosom.[41]

• Our Father counsels and directs us. Listen to Willard again: believers "are tender and foolish in themselves, they have not wisdom enough of their own to order and direct their way; and are therefore easily seduced and cheated by the adversary, who is subtle, and watcheth all advantages against [them]: but God is alwayes giving them his Fatherly advice, warning them of their danger, shewing them a way how to escape it: they have the voice of his Spirit behind them, telling them this is the way, *Isai.* 30.21.; they have the guidance of his most wise counsel to keep them in the right way unto glory, *Psal.* 74.24."[42]

• Our Father offers us spiritual, Christian liberty as His sons and daughters (John 8:36). This liberty

---

40. Willard, *The Child's Portion*, 22.

41. Witsius, *Economy of the Covenants,* 1:449; Girardeau, *Theological Questions,* 493.

42. Willard, *The Child's Portion*, 17–18.

releases us from bondage (Gal. 4:7). It delivers us from the slavish subjection, the servile pedagogy, the condemning power, the intolerable yoke, and the thundering curses of the law as a covenant of works (Gal. 3:13), though not from the law's regulating power.[43] We are not dependent on our obedience to the law for our justification and happiness (Rom. 3:28), but as sons of God—not mercenaries—we obey the law as "a service of love."[44] We who were once "the servants of sin" have been, by adoption, "made free from sin, [and we] became the servants of righteousness" (Rom. 6:17–18).[45]

Expounding John Owen's thought, Sinclair Ferguson writes that "the only freedom a slave could enjoy would be *from* his duty, says Owen, but God's child may enjoy a freedom *in* his duty, since it is grounded in love.... He is not without law to God, but under the law of Christ. The maintenance of liberty for the main-stream Puritans was always dependent upon this paradox."[46]

Christian liberty delivers us from the impugning, condemning, and reigning power of sin (2 Cor.

---

43. *Works of Boston,* 1:625; Cole, *Christ the Foundation of our Adoption,* 352–53.

44. Burroughs, *The Saints' Happiness,* 194.

45. Ridgley, *Commentary on the Larger Catechism,* 2:134.

46. Ferguson, *John Owen on the Christian Life* (Edinburgh: Banner of Truth Trust, 1987), 90; *Works of Owen,* 2:213–15; cf. Ernest Kevan, *The Grace of Law: A Study in Puritan Theology* (Grand Rapids: Baker, 1976), 185–86.

5:29; Rom. 8:1; 6:12), making possible the enjoyment of peace with God as His children. But that liberty must not be abused. As Cole writes, "'Tis a dangerous thing to speak too freely of Christian Liberty, because many under that pretence, allow themselves in very unwarrantable courses, running into excess, laying aside all Moderation, Order and Government of themselves in the use of outward things. Luxury in Diet, Pride in Apparel, &c. can never be justified by the doctrine of Christian Liberty."[47]

Spiritual liberty delivers us from the world and all its powerful temptations, persecutions, and threatenings (1 John 5:4). It delivers us from the bondage of Satan, from hypocrisy and anxiety, and from the traditions of men, so that we may freely bind ourselves to the teaching of God. It grants us liberty to live transparently before God, to serve and love God and His ways with heart, mind, and strength (Ps. 18:1), so that we gladly take His yoke upon us and serve Him with filial obedience each day (1 Peter 1:14), confessing that "this is my Father's world."[48]

• Our Father preserves us and keeps us from falling (Ps. 91:11–12; 1 Peter 1:5). He restores us from every backsliding way, recovering and humbling us, always preventing our hypocrisy.[49] Samuel Willard says,

---

47. Cole, *Christ the Foundation of our Adoption,* 355.

48. Willard, *The Child's Portion,* 23–27.

49. Ridgley, *Commentary on the Larger Catechism,* 2:136.

"Gods Sons in this life are like little Children, always tripping, and stumbling, and falling, and so weak that they could never get up again but for him: but by reasons of his hand that is upon them, his everlasting Arm that is under them. Hence if they fall at any time through incogitancy, or by stumbling at any thing that lies in their way, or through that weakness that attends them, or by Satans malice thrusting at them, he will lift them up again."[50]

• Our Father provides everything that we need as His children, both physically and spiritually (Ps. 34:10; Matt. 6:31–33), and He will protect us from all harm. He will defend us from our enemies—Satan, the world, and our own flesh—and right our wronged cause. He will assist and strengthen us, always lending us a helping hand to carry us through every difficulty and temptation (2 Tim. 4:17). We may safely leave everything in His fatherly hands, knowing that He will never leave us nor forsake us (Heb. 13:5–6). We are children under our Father's special inspection and care (1 Peter 5:7) for the entirety of our earthly pilgrimage, "sealed to the day of redemption" (WCF, XII) in glory, where we will be beyond all danger (Rev. 21:25).[51]

• Our Father gives His angels, as ministering spir-

50. Willard, *The Child's Portion*, 17.

51. Ibid., 16–18; *Works of Boston*, 625.

its, to serve us for good (Ps. 34:7; Heb. 1:14).[52] They guard us and watch for us. Willard calls them "tutelary Angels" who guard and defend us from evil and watch for our good (Ps. 91:11). "They pitch their tents round about [believers], *Psal.* 34.1, they bring down messages of peace from heaven, even answers of their Prayers, *Dan.* 9.23, strengthen and confirm them in their secret conflicts, *Luk.* 22.43, and when they come to die, they are a convoy to carry their Souls home to eternal rest, *Luk.* 16.22."[53]

• Our Father makes death a narrow gate to lead us into everlasting life in heaven.[54] Says Marshall, "The prepared possession which was cast by God from all Eternity, all the Glory of Heaven, such as Eye never saw, nor never entred into the heart of man to conceive of, it is all kept to be the everlasting inheritance of all those that are called the Lords Children."[55]

One day we will be introduced into the full experience of the heavenly life now being enjoyed by our Elder Brother. We will be brought into His immediate presence and be satisfied with His likeness (Ps. 17:15)—likeness in body, in mind, in character. "We shall be like him; for we shall see him as he is"

---

52. *Workes of Perkins*, 1:83, 369.

53. Willard, *The Child's Portion*, 27–28; Granger, *A Looking Glasse for Christians,* [30–31].

54. *Workes of Perkins*, 1:369.

55. *Works of Marshall,* 53.

(1 John 3:2). Then we will be delivered from every remnant of corruption; we will have the glorious liberty of our adoption, the redemption of our bodies, and access to our full inheritance as we bask and share in the glory of our Immanuel who will be all in all (Rom. 8).

———————— ♦ ————————

CHAPTER ELEVEN

The Responsibilities or Duties of Adoption

The Puritans taught that every privilege of adoption has a corresponding responsibility or duty, each of which transforms the way believers think and live. These may be summarized as follows:

• Trust your Father for your every need. Behave as a child of your heavenly Father by living above fear, anxiety, and the vanities of this world. Don't be dejected when you lack many of this world's comforts. Remember that your Father has all power and control in His hands. You will lack no needful thing, and every trial will work for good. "Therefore," Burroughs advises, "when any affliction doth befall thee, do not thou presently let thy heart sink."[1]

Bring all your needs to your Father in prayer and, trusting His care (1 Peter 5:7), leave them with Him, remembering that your Father knows "what things ye

---

1. Burroughs, *The Saints' Happiness*, 197.

have need of, before ye ask him" (Matt. 6:8). Brakel writes, "Make all your needs known to your Father, that is, whatever presses you down, threatens you, and you long to have; do this as intimately as a child would ask his father," in subjection to your Father's will, trusting that He knows best what to give and what to withhold.[2]

• Show childlike reverence, love, and zeal for your Father in everything. Reflect habitually on your Father's great glory and majesty. Stand in awe of Him; render Him praise and thanksgiving in all things. Obey Malachi 1:6: "A son honoureth his father, and a servant his master: if then I be a father, where is mine honour? and if I be a master, where is my fear."[3]

Remember that your holy Father sees everything. Children sometimes commit dreadful acts in the absence of their parents, but your Father is never absent. Anthony Burgess explains: *"There is nothing done in secret, but thy Father seeth it.* There is no heart-pride, no heart-earthlynesse, but thy Father seeth it. There is never a time thou prayest, hearest the word, but thy Father seeth with what form of Spirit it is. Oh therefore if thou art a Son of God, thou wilt discover it in thy whole carriage: a Son

---

2. Brakel, *Christian's Reasonable Service,* 2:436; cf. Willard, *The Child's Portion,* 47.

3. Burroughs, *The Saints' Happiness,* 198.

feareth the frowns of his Father; I dare not do this; my father will be offended; and I, Whither shall I go? Thus the Apostle *Peter, If ye call him Father, passe your sojourning here with fear,* 1 Pet. 1.17."[4]

Thomas Hooker applies this further: "Abdicate and abandon all bad company, all your former sins and lusts, never to resume, or take them into your practice again. [It is] a shame for us, who are heirs apparent to the kingdom of heaven, to be groveling among things of this life with others."[5]

Rather, let childlike reverence overflow in love to your Father — a love that constrains you to employ all the means of grace, to obey His commands, and to work for Him. Burroughs writes, "Do all you do out of love, be not mercenary. A servant doth not care to do anything any further than he may be paid for it, but a child doth not so; he doth what he doth out of love. Oh that we could bring all our obedience to be out of love to God."

Such love, Burroughs continues, will lead to zeal for your Father's glory: "A child would be zealous for the honour of his father," he says, so "when you see your Father struck at, that should make your spirits boil within you."[6]

4. Burgess, *Spiritual Refining,* 239.
5. Hooker, *The Christian's Two Chief Lessons,* 169.
6. Burroughs, *The Saints' Happiness,* 199.

• Submit to your Father in every providence. When He visits you with the rod, don't resist or murmur. Don't immediately respond by saying, "'I am not a child of God, God is not my Father, God deals harshly with me; if He were my Father, He would have compassion on me; He would then deliver me from this grievous and especially this sinful cross'— to speak thus does not befit the nature of an upright child," writes Brakel. Rather, "it is fitting for a child to be quiet, to humbly submit, and to say, 'I will bear the indignation of the LORD, because I have sinned against him'" (Mic. 7:9).[7]

Burgess asks, "What is the ground of all our impatience, discontent, and trouble against Gods dispensations? Is it not because we look not upon him as so wise, and so potent a Father? Who can do it better? Can the Artificer know when his gold hath been enough in the furnace, and he will not let it stay a moment longer: and shall not God know when he hath chastised thee enough: If thou hadst a Child-like disposition, thou wouldst say, although all I feel be bitter, yet he is a Father still. I have been an ill Child, and this makes him a Good Father in chastising."[8]

• Obey and imitate your Father, and love His image-bearers. Strive to be like Him, to be holy as He is holy, to be loving as He is loving. We are to be imitators of

---

7. Brakel, *Christian's Reasonable Service,* 2:437.
8. Burgess, *Spiritual Refining,* 239.

God (Eph. 5:1) to show that we bear the family likeness. Gordon Cooke writes, "This, of course, is hard for children who are adopted. By nature we are children of another family, and it is those family traits that more often come to the surface. Mortification of sin then is in keeping with our standing as children of God."[9]

We are to love the Father's image wherever we see it. Willard writes, "The Saints are living Images of the Lord, we may see in them, not only the likeness to, but the shining reflection of his communicated perfections: Hence we should love the Saints."[10] We are to live as God's children in mutual love and patience with each other, having the same Father, Elder Brother, and indwelling Spirit. "It is enough that the children of the world wrangle one with another and fight; let not those that profess God to be their Father, oh let them not in the presence of their Father wrangle and fight one with another, for certainly the Spirit of God cannot bear it," Burroughs concludes.[11]

---

9. Cooke, "The Doctrine of Adoption and the Preaching of Jeremiah Burroughs," 37.

10. Willard, *The Child's Portion*, 43.

11. Burroughs, *The Saints' Happiness,* 200. Burroughs himself was known for his conciliatory spirit. "If all the Episcopalians had been like Archbishop Ussher," wrote Richard Baxter, "all the Presbyterians like Mr Stephen Marshall, and all the Independents like Jeremiah Burroughs, the breaches of the church would soon have been healed" (quoted in James Reid, *Memoirs*

Love among the believing family of God is essential, the Puritans taught. Listen to Boston: "O how unnatural are the jarrings and discords among those that profess to be of the same family of heaven! Our heavenly Father setting his children on their way home together, says, as Joseph said to his brethren, 'See that ye fall not out by the way,' Gen. xlv. 24. Lay by all feuds and discords among yourselves, forgive as ye would be forgiven."[12]

Nothing is more destructive in the church and to the world than the lack of love among believers. Christianity then appears to be a façade, a curse, a deception (1 John 2:9–11; 3:11–18; 4:7–21). Believers ought to be gentle with each other, especially with beginners in grace who are stumbling. They ought to show the meekness of Christ to their spiritual brothers and sisters, as Paul did to the Corinthians. They ought to be promoters of love and unity in the family of God.[13]

• Resist every hindrance that keeps you from relishing your Father's adopting grace. Simon Ford devotes thirty pages to telling us how to do that. Here are the main hindrances he urges us strenuously to oppose:

---

of the Westminster Divines [Edinburgh: Banner of Truth Trust, 1982], 2:81).

12. *Works of Boston*, 1:628–29.

13. Erroll Hulse, "Recovering the Doctrine of Adoption," *Reformation Today* 105 (1988):13–14.

- A secret *murmuring* frame of spirit against Gods present dispensations towards thee; as if God dealt very hardly and contrary to his wonted course with thee.

- A kind of *delight in complaining* against thy self, and taking Satans part many times in bearing false witness against thy own soul.

- An *unthankful denyal* of the works of Gods sanctifying spirit in the heart.

- An unwarrantable *thrusting off* those promises and comfortable truths which God in the Ministry of the Word or otherwise brings home to our condition, and *snatching* greedily at all the terrible places of Scripture and denunciations of wrath as our portion.

- A groundlesse *surmising* of an irrecoverablenesse in our condition from such and such *threatenings of Scripture* as concerne us not.

- *Keeping Satans counsel.*

- Secret *tempting of God*, and *dependence* upon such means and such men for *peace*, and *limiting* God to such and such a time, and *resolving* not to wait on God beyond that time, or not to expect it from any other meanes.

- A sinfull *ambition of self-preparations* for comfort and peace: were I so much humbled, saith the poor soul, so kindly and ingenuously affected with my sins; could I recover of this deadnesse, and flatnesse of spirit into any measure of livelinesse and spiritualnesse in my performances; then I would believe comfort, and assurance of God's love belonged to me; but that a soul so little, so legally broken as I am, so barren, saplesse, lifeless, spiritless in all my services should have any share in Christ, any title to the Covenant of Grace, any part or portion with the Saints of God, I cannot, I will not believe.

- Giving too much way to *prejudices against God,* and his love, from *present sense and feeling.*

- *Slacknesse* and *remissnesse in* (occasioned by successelessenesse of) Ordinances and Duties.

- *Over-scrupulousness, and scepticall-question-fulnesse.*[14]

• Engage in your Father's work. Lika a son wants to go his father's way, do his father's will, and engage in his father's work, so true spiritual sons of the heavenly Father want to discipline themselves and channel their energies into the structures and work that God has for us in the fellowship of His church. Like Christ, our elder Brother, we must be about our Father's business, remembering that the night is coming when no man can work (John 9:4).

• Rejoice in being in your Father's presence. Delight in communing with Him. Burgess points out that "a Son delights to have letters from his Father, to have discourse about him, especially to enjoy his presence." How, then, "art thou affected in praying, in hearing, in all religious duties? They are a constant

---

14. Ford, *The Spirit of Bondage and Adoption,* 258–87.

burthen and trouble to thee; this argueth thee to be no son of God. Let not therefore vain delusions carry thee aside: It is not thy coming to Church, thy standing within Gods Courts, that demonstrates thee to be of God; but it is an heavenly and spiritual joy in these approaches."[15]

In heaven, this joy will be full; our adoption will then be perfected (Rom. 8:23). Then we will enter into the Father's "presence and palace," where we will be "everlastingly enjoying, delighting, and praising God."[16] Let us wait and long for that time, as children who eagerly anticipate our full inheritance, when the Triune God shall be our all in all.[17]

---

15. Burgess, *Spiritual Refining,* 240.

16. *Works of Manton,* 12:125.

17. Drake, *Puritan Sermons,* 5:342; cf. Willard, *The Child's Portion,* 71.

CHAPTER TWELVE

— ♦ —

Motives for Pursuing the Consciousness of Adoption

The Puritans set forth numerous motives for pursuing a conscious sense of one's adoption, many of which overlap with privileges already expounded. Here are several motives not yet covered adequately:

(1) *Peace and comfort.* William Perkins writes, "If we would haue true peace and comfort in euery estate, whether aduersitie or prosperitie, let vs labour for the knowledge of our adoption. This will be our ioy in want, in wealth, in bondage, in freedome, in sickenesse, in health, in life, & in death."[1]

A sense of our adoption, says Thomas Manton, provides "peace of conscience—a rest from those troubled and unquiet thoughts which otherwise would perplex us."[2] The sense of knowing we belong

---

1. *Workes of Perkins*, 3:382 (2).
2. *Works of Manton*, 12:119.

to God's family ought to motivate us to pursue adoption.

(2) *Experience of God's love.* The child who appreciates his parents' love in adopting him is a grateful child. As he grows in years, tears of joy more often fill his eyes as he reflects on that love in contrast to what he has deserved. So we should feel about the love of the Triune God toward us. As Thomas Watson says, "God did not adopt us when we were bespangled with the jewels of holiness, and had the angels' glory upon us; but when we were black as Ethiopians, diseased as lepers, then it was the time of love."[3] Here is a summary of Stephen Marshall's thoughts on this grand subject:

> How the love of the Father ought to motivate us toward a greater realization of our adoption! People on earth often adopt children because they have none or because those they have are not pleasing them so that their name will not be perpetuated well. But why did the Father condescend from all eternity to choose you, a mere worm at best, yes, an enemy by nature, when He had a perfect, devoted Son from eternity?
>
> How the love of the Son ought to motivate us toward a greater realization of our adoption! People on earth are seldom troubled that they have no more brothers or sisters to share in their inheritance; in fact, they often fear that there are too many. But the Son of God came to this earth to

---

3. Watson, *A Body of Practical Divinity,* 157.

give His own blood to "purchase poor worms to be Coheirs, and a Brother with himself, and that he would likewise give himself to thee as a Brother, that thou shouldest be one mystically with him."

How the love of the Spirit ought to motivate us toward a greater realization of our adoption! How amazing it is that the Spirit would condescend to indwell us, "to alter & frame our cursed natures, and (as need shall require) to be a constant supplication of comfort and refreshing to us."

"Here is love the like was never heard of, that the Lord should rear poor Worms, and let such a work pass upon them, to make them the Sons of God."[4]

(3) *Readiness for duty.* When believers know they are adopted of God, "they serve God with a free spirit; the holy life is carried on with more sweetness and success; not by compulsion, but with ready mind," writes Manton. "Men are under shackles and bondage if they have not the spirit of adoption; they drive on heavily, have not largeness of heart, and love to God, heaven, and holiness." But, by the grace of adoption, "when the heart is suited to the work, there needs no other urgings; but if we force a course of religion upon ourselves, contrary to our own inclination, all is harsh, and ingrate, and cannot hold long."[5]

(4) *Liberty in prayer.* The Spirit of adoption provides unspeakable help in prayer (Zech. 12:10). "That

---

4. *Works of Marshall,* 56–58.

5. *Works of Manton,* 12:119.

Spirit which cometh from the grace and free favour of God, stirs up childe-like addresses to God, Rom. viii. 26; Jude 21," writes Manton. "Without this, our prayers are but a vain babbling."[6]

(5) *Victory over Satan.* Listen to Perkins again: "The Deuils drift is to ouerthrow this perswasion [of being adopted by God] in vs, and therefore our endeauour must be, to confirme and settle our hearts herein" (2 Peter 1:10). Perkins goes on: "We cannot doe the Deuill a greater pleasure than to neglect the getting of this assurance; for hereupon he will take occasion (specially in time of distresse) fearefully and daungerously to seek to breake the necke of our soules; he cares not much otherwaies what men professe, and what knowledge and other common gifts of the spirit they haue, so that they want this blessed assurance."[7]

We must live by hope, not by "present sense," remembering, as Willard wisely observes, "It is the delight of Satan to be keeping the thoughts of the Children of God looking, and poring upon their present sinful and sorrowful condition, that they may be held under discouragement by thinking themselves miserable, but we live by hope."[8]

---

6. Ibid.

7. *Workes of Perkins*, 3:382 (2nd pagination).

8. Willard, *The Child's Portion*, 70.

♦

CHAPTER THIRTEEN

Warning, Invitation, and Comfort

The classic Puritan statement on adoption in the Westminster Standards leaves much unsaid. The Puritans are by no means exhaustive in their doctrine of spiritual adoption. For example, they have not adequately addressed the centrality of sonship in biblical doctrine nor as an organizing principle for understanding salvation along the lines that Sinclair Ferguson suggests.[1]

Nevertheless, the Puritans teach us a great deal more about spiritual adoption and its transforming power than has been acknowledged. They teach us the importance of fleeing from sin and pursuing a conscious sense of our adoption.[2] They show us, as Packer helpfully summarizes, that our adoption helps

---

1. Cf. Ferguson, "The Reformed Doctrine of Sonship," 84–87.

2. *Workes of Perkins*, 3:205: "Wouldest thou know thy selfe to be the childe of God? Remember then to purge thy heart and life from all sinne, for thence floweth true vunderstanding, and thereupon God will certifie thy conscience of thine election and

us better grasp the ministry of the Holy Spirit, the power of gospel holiness, our own assurance of faith, the solidity of the Christian family, and the glory of the Christian hope.[3]

The Puritans also warn us of the danger of remaining a member of Satan's family—especially while under the means of grace. "Many a gospel-call has sounded in your ears, sinner," writes Thomas Boston; "hast thou not come away on the call? Then thou art yet a child of the devil, Acts xiii. 10. and therefore an heir of hell and of wrath." When the unbeliever objects, Boston responds: "Whose image dost thou bear? Holiness is God's image, unholiness the devil's. Thy dark heart and unholy life plainly tell the family thou art of."[4]

As strongly as the Puritans admonish, so strongly they invite. Willard writes, "What do you think of it, [you] who have been often invited in the Gospel to embrace [Christ]? Will not [adoption] present him before you as one worth the entertaining? Receive him by a true Faith, and he will make you, not only Friends, but Children unto God." Willard then goes on to say that if we would be honorable, possess spir-

---

reconciliation; but if thou suffer thy selfe to liue in sinne, thou maist long waite for this certificate, and neuer haue it."

3. Packer, *Knowing God*, 198–207.

4. *Works of Boston*, 1:627; cf. Mather, *The Sealed Servants of our God, Appearing with Two Witnesses*, 23–28.

itual riches, and enjoy divine protection, we need to enter God's family by faith.[5]

Above all, the Puritans use the truth of adoption to transform God's needy children through powerful comforts. Thomas Hooker shows how adoption comforts them in the face of their unworthiness, outward poverty, the contempt of the world, infirmities, afflictions, persecutions, and dangers.[6] When oppressed with sin, buffeted by Satan, enticed by the world, or alarmed by fears of death, believers are to take refuge in their precious, heavenly Father, saying with Willard, "Am I not still a Child? And if so, then I am sure, that though he correct me (and I deserve it, nor will I refuse to submit my self patiently unto it) yet he cannot take away his loving kindness from me."[7]

Willard concludes: "Be always comforting of your selves with the thoughts of your Adoption: Draw your comforts at this tap, fetch your consolations from this relation; be therefore often chewing upon the precious priviledges of it, and make them your rejoicing. Let this joy out-strip the verdure of every other joy. Let this joy dispel the mists of every sorrow, and clear up your souls in the midst of all troubles and difficulties" as you await heavenly glory, where you will live out your perfect adoption by forever com-

5. Willard, *The Child's Portion*, 34–42; cf. Mather, *The Sealed Servants of our God, Appearing with Two Witnesses*, 28–36.

6. Hooker, *The Christian's Two Chief Lessons*, 170–74.

7. Willard, *The Child's Portion*, 51–52.

muning with the Triune God. There you will "dwel at the fountain, and swim for ever in those bankless, and bottomless Oceans of Glory."[8]

---

8. Ibid., 54, 66–70.

Bibliography

Ames, William. *The Marrow of Theology*. Translated and edited by John D. Eusden. Boston: Pilgrim Press, 1968, 164–67.

A practical consideration of the saints sonship. In a discourse upon the fourth chapter of the Galatians, vers. 6. London: Robert Ibbitson, 1656.

Baird, Samuel J. "The Fatherhood of God." *Presbyterian Quarterly* 5 (1891): 350–62.

Barclay, George. *Essays: on Doctrinal, Experimental, and Prophetical Subjects*. Irvine: for the author, and sold by Waugh and Innes, et al., 1828, 177–206.

Barr, James. "Abba Isn't Daddy." *Journal of Theological Studies* 39 (1988): 28–47.

Bates, William. *The Whole Works of the Rev. W. Bates, D.D.* Edited by W. Farmer. Reprint, Harrisonburg, Va.: Sprinkle, 1990, 4:299–301.

Beattie, Francis R. *The Presbyterian Standards: An Exposition of the Westminster Confession of Faith and Catechisms*. Richmond, Va.: Presbyterian Committee of Publication, 1896, 212–16.

Beeke, Joel R. *The Quest for Full Assurance: The Legacy of Calvin and His Successors*. Edinburgh: Banner of Truth Trust, 1999, 60–68, 142–47, 180–85, 233–34.

Berry, Stephen R. "'Sons of God': An Examination of the Doctrine of Adoption in the Thought of John Lafayette Girardeau." Unpublished paper submitted to systematic theology department, Reformed Theological Seminary, Jackson, Miss., 1994.

Binning, Hugh. *The Works of the Rev. Hugh Binning, M.A.* Edited by M. Leishman. Reprint, Ligonier, Pa.: Soli Deo Gloria, 1992, 253–55.

Blekkink, Evert J. *The Fatherhood of God Considered from Six Inter-Related Standpoints*. Grand Rapids: Eerdmans, 1942.

Boice, James Montgomery. *Foundations of the Christian Faith: A Comprehensive & Readable Theology*. Downers Grove, Ill.: InterVarsity Press, 1986, 441–48.

Booth, Abraham. *The Reign of Grace*. Swengel, Pa.: Reiner, 1968, 189–98.

Boston, Thomas. *The Complete Works of the Late Rev. Thomas Boston, Ettrick*. Edited by Samuel M'Millan. Reprint, Stoke-on-Trent, UK: Tentmaker Publications, 2002, 1:612–53, 2:15–27.

Box, G. H. "Adoption." In *Encyclopedia of Religion and Ethics*. Edited by James Hastings. Edinbrugh: T. & T. Clark, 1908, 1:105–115.

Boyce, James P. *Abstract of Systematic Theology*. Reprint, Hanford, Calif.: den Dulk Christian Foundation, n.d., 404–409.

Brakel, Wilhelmus à. *The Christian's Reasonable Service*. Translated by Bartel Elshout. Edited by Joel R. Beeke. Grand Rapids: Reformation Heritage Books, 1999, 2:415–38; 3:486–87.

Breckinridge, Robert J. *The Knowledge of God, Subjectively Considered*. New York: Robert Carter & Brothers, 1859, 178–202.

Brooks, Thomas. *The Works of Thomas Brooks*. Reprint, Edinburgh: Banner of Truth Trust, 2001, 4:419–20.

Brown, John (of Haddington). *An Essay towards an easy, plain, practical, and extensive Explication of the Assembly's Shorter Catechism.* New York: Robert Carter & Brothers, 1849, 162–65.

_____. *The Systematic Theology of John Brown of Haddington.* Grand Rapids: Reformation Heritage Books, 2002, 393–97.

Bruce, Archibald. "St. Paul's Conception of Christianity: 10. Adoption." In *The Expositor,* 4th series, 8 (1893).

Buchanan, James. *The Doctrine of Justification.* Reprint, Edinburgh: Banner of Truth Trust, 1991, 210–11, 261–64.

Bull, George. *A Discourse Concerning the Spirit of God in the Faithful; how, and in what Manner it doth bear Witness with their Spirits, that they are the Children of God; and what Degree of Hope or Persuasion concerning their Adoption, this Witness of the Spirit doth ordinarily produce in the Faithful.* Boston: Thomas Fleet, 1740.

Burgess, Anthony. *CXLV Expository Sermons Upon the whole 17th Chapter of the Gospel According to John.* London: Abraham Miller for Thomas Underhill, 1656.

_____. *Spiritual Refining: or A Treatise of Grace and Assurance.* London: A. Miller for Thomas Underhill, 1652, 237–43.

Burke, Trevor J. "Adoption and the Spirit in Romans 8." *Evangelical Quarterly* 70 (1998): 311–24.

_____. "The Characteristics of Paul's Adoptive-Sonship *(Huiothesia)* Motif." *Irish Biblical Studies* 17 (1995): 62–74.

_____. "Pauline Adoption: A Sociological Approach." *Evangelical Quarterly* 73 (2001): 119–34.

Burris, Thomas S. "The Meaning of *Huiothesia* in the New Testament." Th.M. thesis, Dallas Theological Seminary, 1970.

Burroughs, Jeremiah. *The Saints' Happiness, Delivered in Divers Lectures on the Beatitudes.* Reprint, Beaver Falls, Pa.: Soli Deo Gloria, 1988, 193–202.

Byrne, Brendan. *'Sons of God'—'Seed of Abraham': A Study of the Idea of the Sonship of God of All Christians in Paul Against the Jewish Background.* Rome: Biblical Institute, 1979.

Calvin, John. *Institutes of the Christian Religion.* Edited by John T. McNeill. Translated by Ford Lewis Battles. 2 vols. Philadelphia: Westminster Press, 1960.

Candlish, Robert S. *Discourses bearing upon the Sonship and Brotherhood of Believers and other kindred subjects.* Edinburgh: Adam and Charles Black, 1872.

_____. *The Fatherhood of God.* 2nd ed. Edinburgh: Adam and Charles Black, 1865.

Charnock, Stephen. *The Complete Works of Stephen Charnock.* Edinburgh: James Nichol, 1865, 3:90.

Cole, Thomas. *A Discourse of Christian Religion, in Sundry Points... Christ the Foundation of our Adoption, from Gal. 4.5.* London: for Will. Marshall, 1698.

Cook, James I. "The Conception of Adoption in the Theology of Paul." In *Saved by Hope: Essays in Honor of Richard C. Oudersluys,* edited by James I. Cook. Grand Rapids: Eerdmans, 1978, 133–44.

Cooke, Gordon. "The Doctrine of Adoption and the Preaching of Jeremiah Burroughs." In *Eternal Light, Adoption and Livingstone.* Congregational Studies Conference Papers, 1998 (published by the Evangelical Fellowship of Congregational Churches).

Cooper, John W. *Our Father in Heaven: Christian Faith and Inclusive Language.* Grand Rapids: Baker, 1998.

Cotton, John. *An Exposition of First John.* Reprint, Evansville, Ind.: Sovereign Grace Publishers, 1962.

Crabb, John. *A Testimony concerning the VVorks of the Living God. Shewing how the mysteries of his workings hath worked many wayes in and amongst mankind. Or, The knowledge of God revealed, which shews the way from the bondage of darkness into the liberty of the Sons of God.* London: John Gain, 1682.

Crawford, Thomas. *The Fatherhood of God Considered in Its General and Special Aspects and Particularly in Relation to the Atonement with a Review of Recent Speculations on the Subject.* 3rd ed. Edinburgh: William Blackwood and Sons, 1868.

Criswell, W. A. *Great Doctrines of the Bible, Volume 5: Soteriology.* Grand Rapids: Zondervan: 1985, 106–114.

DeJonge, M. "The Son of God and the Children of God in the Fourth Gospel." In *Saved by Hope: Essays in Honor of Richard C. Oudersluys*, edited by James I. Cook, 44–63. Grand Rapids: Eerdmans, 1978.

Dick, John. *Lectures on Theology.* Philadelphia: J. Whetham & Son, 1841, 2:224–33.

Dickinson, Jonathan. *The Witness of the Spirit. A sermon preached at Newark in New-Jersey, May 7th. 1740. Wherein is distinctly shewn, in what way and manner the Spirit himself beareth witness to the adoption of the children of God.* Boston: S. Kneeland and T. Green, 1740.

Dickson, David. *Truth's Victory over Error.* Reprint, Edinburgh: Banner of Truth, 2007, 76–77.

Donner, Herbert. "Adoption oder Legitimation? Erwägungen zur Adoption im Alten Testament auf dem Hintergrund der altorientalischen Rechte." *Oriens Antiquus* 8 (1969): 87–119.

Dorman, Robert C. "A Study of Paul's Use of *Huiothesia:* Its Background, Development, and Importance Concerning Spiritual Adoption." Th.M. thesis, Covenant Theological Seminary, St. Louis, 1997.

Douty, Norman F. *Union with Christ.* Swengel, Pa.: Reiner, 1973, 174–84.

Downame, George. *A Treatise of Ivstification.* London: Felix Kyngston for Nicolas Bourne, 1633, 239–42.

Drake, Roger. "The Believer's Dignity and Duty Laid Open, in the High Birth wherewith he is Privileged, and the Honourable Employment to which he is Called." In *Puritan Sermons 1659-1689: Being the Morning Exercises at Cripplegate, St. Giles in the Fields, and in Southwark by Seventy-five Ministers of the Gospel in or near London.* Reprint, Wheaton, Ill.: Richard Owen Roberts, 1981, 5:328–44.

Drexel, Jeremias. *A Spiritual Repository containing Godly meditations demonstrated by 12 signs of our adoption to eternal glory.* Translated by R. W. London: R. B., 1676.

Dwight, Timothy. *Theology: Explained and Defended, in a Series of Sermons.* Middletown, Conn.: Clark & Lyman, 1818, 3:181–93.

Ebel, Frank J., Jr. "The Christian's Filial Relationship to God." Th.M. thesis, Dallas Theological Seminary, 1957.

Evans, Robert Wilson. *Parochial Sermons preached in the Parish Church of Heversham, Westmoreland.* London: Francis & John Rivington, 1846, 1–8.

Feigin, Samuel. "Some Cases of Adoption in Israel." *Journal of Biblical Literature* 50 (1931): 186–200.

Ferguson, Sinclair B. *Children of the Living God*. Edinburgh: Banner of Truth Trust, 1989.

_____. *The Holy Spirit*. Downers Grove, Ill.: InterVarsity Press, 1996, 182–86.

_____. *Know Your Christian Life: A Theological Introduction*. Downers Grove, Ill: InterVarsity Press, 1981, 82–91.

_____. *John Owen on the Christian Life*. Edinburgh: Banner of Truth Trust, 1987, 88–91.

_____. "The Reformed Doctrine of Sonship." In *Pulpit and People: Essays in Honour of William Still on his 75th Birthday*, edited by Nigel M. de S. Cameron and Sinclair B. Ferguson. Edinburgh: Rutherford House Books, 1986, 81–88.

Fishburn, J.F. *The Fatherhood of God and the Victorian Family: The Social Gospel*. Philadelphia: Fortress, 1981.

Fisher, James. *The Assembly's Shorter Catechism Explained, by way of Question and Answer*. Reprint, Lewes, East Sussex: Berith Publications, 1998, 184–87.

Flavel, John. *The Works of John Flavel*. Edinburgh: Banner of Truth Trust, 1997, 6:197–99.

Fong, Ken. *Secure in God's Embrace*. Downers Grove, Ill.: InterVarsity Press, 2003.

Forbes, John. *A Letter for resolving this Question: How a Christian man may discerne the testimonie of Gods spirit, from the testimonie of his owne spirit, in witnessing his Adoption*. Middelburg: Richard Schilders, 1616.

Ford, Simon. *The Spirit of Bondage and Adoption: Largely*

and Practically handled, with reference to the way and manner of working both those Effects; and the proper Cases of Conscience belonging to them both. London: T. Maxey, for Sa. Gellibrand, 1655.

Franchino, T. Scott. "*Yios* and *Teknon* in the Doctrine of Adoption: Romans 8." Th.M. thesis, Grace Theological Seminary, 1984.

Frey, Joseph Samuel C. F. *A Course of Lectures on the Scripture Types with a Few Select Sermons.* New York: D. Fanshaw, 1841, 2:291–312.

G., M. *The Glorious Excellencie of the Spirit of Adoption.* London: Jane Coe, for Henry Overton, 1645.

Gadsby, John. *Slavery, Adoption, and Redemption: Biblically, Orientally, and Personally Considered.* Reprint, New Ipswich, N.H.: Pietan, 1994.

Garner, David B. "Adoption in Christ." Ph.D. dissertation, Westminster Theological Seminary, 2002.

_____. "Irenaeus: Founding Father of Adoption Theology." Unpublished paper, Westminster Theological Seminary, Philadelphia, 1999.

Gill, John. *A Complete Body of Doctrinal and Practical Divinity.* Reprint, Paris, Ark.: Baptist Standard Bearer, 1987, 201–203, 518–25.

Gillespie, George. *A Treatise of Miscellany Questions.* Edinburgh: Gedeon Lithgovv, for George Svvintuun, 1649.

Girardeau, John L. *Discussion of Theological Questions.* Edited by George A. Blackburn. Reprint, Harrisonburg, Va.: Sprinkle Publications, 1986, 428–521.

Gladden, W. "The Fatherhood of God as a Theological Factor." *The Homiletic Review* 37 (1899): 201–208.

Goodwin, Thomas. *The Works of Thomas Goodwin.* Reprint, Grand Rapids: Reformation Heritage Books, 2006, 1:83–102.

Gouge, William. *A Gvide to Goe to God: or, An explanation of the perfect Patterne of Prayer, The Lords Prayer*, 2nd ed. London: G.M. for Edward Brewster, 1636, 10–21.

Granger, Thomas. *A Looking-Glasse for Christians. Or, The Comfortable Doctrine of Adoption*. London: William Iones, 1620.

Griffith, Howard. "'The First Title of the Spirit': Adoption in Calvin's Soteriology." *Evangelical Quarterly* 73 (2001): 135–53.

Grudem, Wayne. *Systematic Theology: An Introduction to Biblical Doctrine*. Grand Rapids: Zondervan, 1994, 736–45.

Hawker, Robert. "The Adopted Child." In *The Works of the Rev. Robert Hawker, D.D.* London: for Ebenezer Palmer, 1831, 10:29–42.

Henry, Matthew. *The Complete Works of the Rev. Matthew Henry*. Reprint, Grand Rapids: Baker, 1979, 2:209–10

Heidelberg Catechism, Q. 33.

Hodge, A. A. *Outlines of Theology*. Reprint, Edinburgh: Banner of Truth Trust, 1986, 515–19.

_____. *The Westminster Confession of Faith: A Commentary*. Reprint, Edinburgh: Banner of Truth Trust, 2002, 191–93.

Hoekema, Anthony A. *Saved by Grace*. Grand Rapids: Eerdmans, 1989, 185–87.

Hooker, Thomas. *The Christians Tvvo Chiefe Lessons*. London: T. B[adger] for P. Stephens and C. Meredith, at the Golden Lion in S. Pauls Churchyard, 1640. Re-

    print, Ames, Iowa: International Outreach, 2002,
    159–73.

Hopkins, Ezekiel. *The Works of Ezekiel Hopkins*. Edited by
    Charles W. Quick. Reprint, Morgan, Pa.: Soli Deo
    Gloria, 1997, 2:120–21, 569–76; 3:198–99.

Houston, Thomas. *The Adoption of Sons, Its Nature,
    Spirit, Privileges, and Effects: A Practical and Ex-
    perimental Treatise*. Edinburgh: Alex. Gardner,
    Paisley, 1872.

Hughes, Edwin Holt. *God's Family*. Cincinnati: Abingdon
    Press, 1926.

Hulse, Erroll. *The Believer's Experience*. Grand Rapids:
    Zondervan, 1980, 97–109.

_____. "Recovering the Doctrine of Adoption." *Refor-
    mation Today* 105 (1988): 5–14.

Irons, Joseph. "Adoption." *Zion's Witness* 106 (May 1964):
    250–54.

Jarrel, W. A. "Adoption Not in the Bible Salvation." *The Re-
    view and Expositor* 15 (1918): 459–69.

Jeremias, Joachim. *Abba: Studien zur neutestamentlichen
    Theologie und Zeitgeschichte*. Göttingen: Vanden-
    Hoeck & Ruprecht, 1966, 15–80.

_____. *The Central Message of the New Testament*.
    New York: Charles Scribner's Sons, 1965, 9–30.

Johnston, Mark. G. *Child of a King: The Biblical Doctrine
    of Sonship*. Fearn, Rosshire: Christian Focus, 1997.

Kelly, Douglas. "Adoption: An Underdeveloped Heritage of
    the Westminster Standards." *Reformed Theologi-
    cal Review* 52 (1993): 110–20.

Kennedy, D. James. *Truths that Transform*. Old Tappan,
    N.J.: Revell, 1974, 91–98.

Kennedy, H. "The Regulative Value for the Pauline Theol-
    ogy of the Conception of Christian Sonship." In *The*

Expositor, 8th series, 11 (1916): 447–63; 12 (1916): 26–37.

Kennedy, John. *Man's Relations to God.* Edinburgh: John Mclaren, 1869.

King, S.A. "The Grace of Adoption." *Union Seminary Magazine* 22 (1910): 30–35.

Law, Thomas H. "The Grace of Adoption." *The Southern Presbyterian Review* 30 (1879): 275–88.

Leigh, Edward. *A Treatise of Divinity.* London, 1646, 510–11.

Lidgett, J. Scott. *The Fatherhood of God in Christian Truth and Life.* Edinburgh: T & T Clark, 1902.

Lloyd-Jones, Martyn. *God the Holy Spirit.* Wheaton, Ill.: Crossway, 2000, 187–89.

Lyall, Francis. "Roman Law in the Writings of Paul—Adoption." *Journal of Biblical Literature* 88 (1969): 458–66.

_____. *Slaves, Citizens, Sons: Legal Metaphors in the Epistles.* Grand Rapids: Zondervan, 1984, 67–100.

M'Cheyne, Robert Murray. *A Basket of Fragments.* Reprint, Inverness: Christian Focus, 1975, 40–43.

Manton, Thomas. *The Complete Works of Thomas Manton, D.D.* London: James Nisbet, 1870, 1:33–57; 10:116–21; 12:111–39.

Marshall, Stephen. *The Works of Mr Stephen Marshall, The First Part, [section 2:] The High Priviledge of Beleevers. They are the Sons of God.* London: Peter and Edward Cole, 1661.

Martin, Hugh. "Candlish's Cunningham Lectures." *British and Foreign Evangelical Review* 14 (1865): 720–87.

Marvin, Danny R. "John's Use of *Uios* and *Teknon* Especially in the Constructions *Uios Theou* and *Tekna*

Theou." Th.M. thesis, Western Conservative Baptist Seminary, Portland, Ore., 1979.

Mather, Cotton. *The Sealed Servants of our God, Appearing with Two Witnesses, to produce a Well-Established Assurance of their being the Children of the Lord Almighty or, the Witness of the Holy Spirit, with the Spirit of the Beleever, to his Adoption of God; briefly and plainly Described.* Boston: Daniel Henchman, 1727.

Matthew, James. "The Doctrine of Sonship and the Sonship of Believers." *The Theological Review and the Free Church College Quarterly* 2 (1886): 18–31.

Mawhinney, Allen. "Baptism, Servanthood and Sonship." *Westminster Theological Journal* 49 (1987): 35–64.

_____. "The Family of God: One Model for the Church of the 90s." *Presbyterion* 19, no. 2 (Fall 1993): 77–96.

_____. "God as Father: Two Popular Theories Reconsidered." *Journal of the Evangelical Theological Society* 31 (1988): 181–189.

_____. "*Huiothesia* in the Pauline Epistles: Its Background, Use, and Implications." Ph.D. dissertation, Baylor University, 1983.

Meyer, Heinrich. *Critical and Exegetical Hand-book to The Epistle of the Romans.* New York: Funk & Wagnalls, 1889.

Miller, C. John. *Sonship: Discovering Light in the Gospel as Sons and Daughters of God.* Jenkinton, Pa.: World Harvest Mission, 1997.

Miller, John W. *Calling God 'Father': Essays on the Bible, Fatherhood and Culture.* New York: Paulist Press, 1999.

Mitchell, Alex F., and John Struthers, eds. *Minutes of the Sessions of the Westminster Assembly of Divines... (November 1644 to March 1649)*. Reprint, Edmonton: Still Waters Revival Books, 1991.

Mitchell, R. *The Fatherhood of God*. London: Hamilton, Adams, 1879.

Morey, Robert A. *The Saving Work of Christ: Studies in the Atonement*. Sterling, Va.: Grace Abounding Ministries, n.d., 189–97.

Morgan, James. *The Scripture Testimony of the Holy Spirit*. Edinburgh: T. & T. Clark, 1865, 366–74.

Mosebrook, Keith Alan. "The Pauline Doctrine of the Adoption of Believers." Th.M. thesis, Dallas Theological Seminary, 1981.

Murray, John. *Collected Writings 2: Systematic Theology*. Edinburgh: Banner of Truth Trust, 1977, 223–34.

_____. *Redemption Accomplished and Applied*. Grand Rapids: Eerdmans, 1955, 132–40.

Owen, John. *The Works of John Owen*. Edited by William H. Goold. Reprint, London: Banner of Truth Trust, 1966, 2:207–22; 4:265–70; 23:255–76.

Packer, James I. *Keep in Step with the Spirit*. Grand Rapids: Fleming H. Revell, 1984.

_____. *Knowing God*. Downers Grove, Ill.: InterVarsity, 1973, 181–208.

Palmer, Edwin Hartshorn. *Scheeben's Doctrine of Divine Adoption*. Kampen: J. H. Kok, 1953.

Perkins, William. *The Workes of that Famovs and VVorthy Minister of Christ in the Vniuersitie of Cambridge, Mr. William Perkins*. 3 vols. London: Iohn Legatt and Cantrell Ligge, 1612–13.

Peterson, Robert. *Adopted by God: From Wayward Sin-*

ners to Cherished Children. Phillipsburg, N.J.: P & R, 2001.

_____. "Toward a Systematic Theology of Adoption." *Presbyterion* 27, no. 2 (Fall 2001): 120–31.

Petto, Samuel. *The Voice of the Spirit. Or, An essay towards a discoverie of the witnessings of the Spirit.* London: Livewell Chapman, 1654.

Pipa, Joseph A. *The Westminster Confession of Faith Study Book.* Ross-shire, U.K.: Christian Focus Publications, 2005.

Reymond, Robert L. *A New Systematic Theology of the Christian Faith.* Nashville: Thomas Nelson, 1998, 759–62.

Ridgley, Thomas. *Commentary on the Larger Catechism.* Edmonton: Still Waters Revival Books, 1993, 2:131–37.

Riffe, Robert Lee. "A Study of the Figure of Adoption in the Pauline Epistles." Th.M. thesis, Dallas Theological Seminary, 1981.

Roberts, Maurice. "The Doctrine of Adoption." Unpublished paper, delivered at Free Reformed Ministers' Conference in Puslinch, Ontario, 2003.

Rosenmeir, Jesper. "'Clearing the Medium': A Reevaluation of the Puritan Plain Style in Light of John Cotton's *A Practicall Commentary Upon the First Epistle Generall of John.*" *William and Mary Quarterly,* 37, no. 4 (1980): 577–91.

Rutherford, Samuel. *The Covenant of Life Opened, or A Treatise of the Covenant of Grace.* Edinburgh: Andro Anderson, for Robert Broun, 1655.

Scott, James M. *Adoption as Sons of God: An Exegetical Investigation Into the Background of* Huiothesia *in the Pauline Corpus.* Tübingen: J. C. B. Mohr, 1992.

Scudder, Henry. *The Christian's Daily Walk, in holy Security and Peace.* Reprint, Harrisburg, Va.: Sprinkle, 1984.

Selbie, W.B. *The Fatherhood of God.* New York: Charles Scribner's Sons, 1936.

Shaw, Robert. *The Reformed Faith: An Exposition of the Westminster Confession of Faith.* Reprint, Inverness: Christian Focus, 1974, 137–41.

Shepard, Thomas. *The Sincere Convert and The Sound Believer.* Reprint, Morgan, Pa.: Soli Deo Gloria, 1999, 251–55.

Shepherd, Samuel G. "The Pauline Doctrine of Sonship." Ph.D. dissertation, Southern Baptist Theological Seminary, 1951.

Sibbes, Richard. *The excellencie of the Gospell above the law Wherein the liberty of the sonnes of God is shewed. With the image of their graces here, and glory hereafter. Which affords much comfort and great incouragement, to all such as begin timely, and continue constantly in the wayes of God.* London: Tho. Cotes, 1639.

_____. "Yea and Amen; or, Precious Promises." In *Works of Richard Sibbes.* Edinburgh: Banner of Truth Trust, 2001, 4:129–49.

Smail, Thomas A. *The Forgotten Father.* Grand Rapids: Eerdmans, 1980.

Sproul, R. C. *Saved from What?* Wheaton, Ill.: Crossway, 2002, 103–123.

Stibbe, Mark. *From Orphans to Heirs: Celebrating Our Spiritual Adoption.* Oxford: Bible Reading Fellowship, 1999.

Stolt, Birgit. "Martin Luther on God as Father." *Lutheran Quarterly* 8 (1994): 385–95.

Swetnam, James. "On Romans 8:23 and the 'Expectation of Sonship.'" *Biblica* 48 (1967): 102–108.

Tennent, John. "The Nature of Adoption." In *Salvation in Full Color: Twenty Sermons by Great Awakening Preachers*. Edited by Richard Owen Roberts. Wheaton, Ill.: International Awakening Press, 1994, 233–50.

Theron, Daniel J. "'Adoption' in the Pauline Corpus." *Evangelical Quarterly* 28 (1956): 6–14.

Thompson, E. M., ed. *Minutes of the Sessions of the Westminster Assembly of Divines, from August 4, 1643 to April 24, 1652*. 3 vols. Transcript from original in Dr. Williams Library, Queen Square, London. Held at the Library, New College, University of Edinburgh.

Trumper, Tim J. R. "An Historical Study of the Doctrine of Adoption in the Calvinistic Tradition." Ph.D. dissertation, University of Edinburgh, 2001.

_____. "The Metaphorical Import of Adoption: A Plea for Realisation I and II: The Adoption Metaphor in Biblical Usage." *Scottish Bulletin of Evangelical Theology* 14 (1996): 129–45; 15 (1997): 98–115.

Turretin, Francis. *Institutes of Elenctic Theology*. Translated by George Musgrave Giger. Edited by James T. Dennison, Jr. Phillipsburg, N.J.: P & R, 1994, 2:666–69.

Twisse, William. *The Doctrine of the Synod of Dort and Arles, reduced to the practice*. Amsterdam: G. Thorp, 1631.

Twisselman, W. *Die Gotteskindschaft der Christen nach dem Neuen Testament*. Gütersloh: Bertelsmann, 1939.

Ussher, James. *A Body of Divinity: or, The Sum and Substance of Christian Religion*. London: J. D. for Nathaniel Ranew and Jonathan Robinson, 1677, 162–63.

Van der Linde, S. *De Leer van den Heiligen Geest bij Calvijn*. Wageningen: H. Veenman, 1943.

Van Dixhorn, Chad. "The *Sonship* Program, for Revival: A Summary and Critique." *Westminster Theological Journal* 61 (1999): 227–46.

Vellanickal, Matthew. *The Divine Sonship of Christians in the Johannine Writings*. Rome: Biblical Institute, 1977.

Vincent, Thomas. *The Shorter Catechism of the Westminster Assembly Explained and Proved from Scripture*. Reprint, Edinburgh: Banner of Truth Trust, 1980.

Visser't, H. *The Fatherhood of God in an Age of Emancipation*. Philadelphia: Westminster, 1982.

Vos, Johannes G. *The Westminster Larger Catechism: A Commentary*. Phillipsburg: P & R Publishing, 2002, 164–66.

Waite, John. *Of the Creatures Liberation from the Bondage of Corruption, Wherein is Discussed...* [section V]: *And lastly is discussed that glorious libertie of the sonnes of God into which the creature is to be reduced*. York: Tho. Broad, 1650.

Wanamaker, Charles A. "The Son and The Sons of God: A Study in Elements of Paul's Christologial and Soteriological Thought." Ph.D. dissertation, University of Durham, 1980.

Watson, J. *The Fatherhood of God, being the second Hartley Lecture delivered in Leeds, June 1898*. London: Thomas Mitchell, 1899.

Watson, Thomas. *A Body of Divinity in a Series of Sermons on the Shorter Catechism*. London: A. Fullarton, 1845, 155–60.

Webb, Robert Alexander. *Christian Salvation: Its Doctrine and Experience*. Richmond, Va.: Presbyterian Committee of Publication, 1921, 391–405.

_____. "The Fatherhood of God." *Presbyterian Quarterly* 5 (1891): 56–70.

_____. *The Reformed Doctrine of Adoption*. Reprint, Grand Rapids: Eerdmans, 1947.

Wermuth, Robert E. "The Doctrine of Adoption in Paul's Ephesian Letter." Th.M. thesis, Covenant Theological Seminary, St. Louis, 1985.

Westhead, Nigel. "Adoption in the Thought of John Calvin." *Scottish Bulletin of Evangelical Theology* 13 (1995): 102–115.

Westminster Confession of Faith, chapter 12 (see also *Larger Catechism*, Q. 74, and *Shorter Catechism*, Q. 34).

Whaling, Thornton. "Adoption." *Princeton Theological Review* 21 (1923): 223–35.

Widdicombe, Peter. *The Fatherhood of God from Origen to Athanasius*. Oxford: Clarendon, 1994, 223–49.

Willard, Samuel. *The Child's Portion: Or the unseen Glory of the Children of God, Asserted, and proved: Together with several other Sermons Occasionally Preached*. Boston: Samuel Green, to be sold by Samuel Phillips, 1684.

_____. *A Compleat Body of Divinity*. Reprint, New York: Johnson Reprint Corporation, 1969, 482–91.

Wilterdink, G. A. "The Fatherhood of God in Calvin's Thought." *Reformed Review* 30 (Autumn 1976): 9–22.

Witsius, Herman. *The Economy of the Covenants Between God & Man.* Reprint, Kingsburg, Calif.: den Dulk Christian Foundation, 1990, 1:441–68.

Woudenberg, Bernard. "Eternal Adoption." *The Standard Bearer* (September 1, 1990), 475–77.

Wright, C.H.H. *The Fatherhood of God and its Relation to the Person and Work of Christ and the Operations of the Holy Spirit.* Edinburgh: T. & T. Clark, 1867.

Yohn, Rick. *Living Securely in an Unstable World: God's Solution to Man's Dilemma.* Portland, Ore.: Multnomah, 1985, 229–47.

Zachman, Randall C. *The Assurance of Faith: Conscience in the Theology of Martin Luther and John Calvin.* Minneapolis: Fortress Press, 1993.

Scripture Index

Also available from
Reformation Heritage Books

MEET THE
PURITANS

Joel R. Beeke
and
Randall J. Pederson

Meet the Puritans provides a biographical and theological introduction to the Puritans whose works have been reprinted in the last fifty years, and also gives helpful summaries and insightful analyses of those reprinted works. It contains nearly 150 biographical entries, and nearly 700 summaries of reprinted works.

978-1-60178-000-3   Hardback, 935 pages